COLOR BLIND CASTING
Unblurring the Lines

By
Jocelyn A. Brown, PhD

Brown and Sons Publishing
Denver, Colorado

Color Blind Casting: Unblurring the Lines

Copyright © 2008, 2012 by Jocelyn A. Brown, PhD

ISBN-13: 978-1494424602
ISBN-10:1494424606

1. Theatre. 2. Ethnic Studies. 3. Race. 4. Colorblind. 5. Casting. 6. Society. 7. African Americans

First Edition: 2008 *Assessing Colorblind Casting in American Theatre and Society* UMI Proquest OCLC: AAI3303858
Revised Edition: 2012

Brown & Sons Publishing
Denver, Colorado
http://brownandsonspublishing.com

For Malachi Truth Brown and Malia Casey Brown

Preface

Color Blind Theatre: To Be or Not to Be

The theoretical, practical, and political struggle over color blind casting has left theatre practitioners at an impasse. Emotions and artistic investments run high around the issue. Discussions of race had intermittently crept into the field throughout history but overt systematic dialogue did not reach a national level until the mid 1980s. Assessing color blind casting in theatre and offering a proposal for its appropriate use is most relevant in an emerging poly-cultural era.

African American cultural and social development has followed a path of self-definition with aims apart from White American culture. Thus, African American identity concerns need to be more fully considered when weighing the use of this practice. The fact that there is an imbalance in the number of African American theatres in America as well as an imbalance in being able to use color blindness in the reverse – color blind casting projects have primarily used African American artists in White roles - makes it clear that a resolution depends upon balancing out the needs of the two parties who are considered in this treatment. Finally, we know that this is a debate that will not resolve itself without much concerted effort. Many scholars have put a good deal of thought into workable solutions. To my knowledge, no models or prescriptions for reducing the use of color blind practices have been written, although many African Americans artists and scholars have offered informal suggestions. My proposals are based on those suggestions and on the views of some scholars and practitioners who are non-traditionalists.

The first step in being collectively responsible American artists is to begin using accurate and effectual language. Much of what is labeled color blind theatre is in actuality color-conscious theatre. The contradictions point to the futility in using such language. Producer and director Rodney K. Douglas contributed the terms "interracial," "cross-over," and "mixed-race" casting. Douglas' term "mixed race casting" is the most accurate description of a theatre practice that presents and represents a poly-cultural society. There is little room for misinterpretation or for loopholes that would allow American theatres to merely cast an actor of color in a traditional, mainstream production, rather than stage an August Wilson drama. The specificity of the term also allows policy-making bodies, like Equity, the means to measure and gauge the use and effectiveness of its laws and by-laws.

The second step toward resolution is deciding when and where such casting should occur. To summarize, the plan that is suggested to address the question of color blind casting as a practice in American theatre, and to make effective use of what Robert Lieberman calls an "enormously appealing and compelling" idea, entails the following changes:

We can reach a consensus on terminology so that the intention of upholding a culturally balanced American theatre institution can be clearly recognized and reached.

American theatre practitioners should also consider the most impacting situations for presenting such productions, keeping in mind the benefits to the actors and the communities. We can encourage mixed race casting experimental practices *and* ethnic theatre at learning and civic institutions.

Simultaneously, American theatre, as a collective, has a long distance to go with building a more ethnically balanced national institution that does not negate the need for a clearly defined African American, Latino, Asian, or Other theatre. Charting new ground requires an exposure to and an experience with existing ground. Then, we can consider new intercultural/mixed race projects that represent the African American race with all of its cultural expressions rather than merely through skin color.

Jocelyn A. Brown, PhD

TABLE OF CONTENTS

Introduction

The world of theatre is undergoing major transformations since the politics of race began to permeate its environment over fifty years ago. Discussions of race had intermittently crept into the field throughout history but overt systematic dialogue did not reach a national level until the mid 1980s when Actor's Equity Association completed a four year study which addressed policy-making around racial casting. The union found that minorities were underrepresented in the performing arts. Following Equity's report, the Non-Traditional Casting Project created a nationwide forum to explore the theoretical and practical applications of a more race-inclusive theatre society. While major changes in theatre practices were not made following this first foray into race and theatre politics, the idea of a theatre reformation was planted in the minds, if not the practices, of American theatre practitioners. Ten years following the forum, the idea of color blind casting in theatre came under severe scrutiny in the form of a nationally known debate between two key figures in American theatre: playwright August Wilson and theatre critic Robert Brustein. African American artistry and mainstream artistry (what many would consider White American) became the major players in the debate, in part, due to the initial impetus of the argument – August Wilson's article "The Ground On Which I Stand," which appeared in the Theatre Communication Group's September 1996 issue. Wilson wrote at length about the need to conceptualize and cultivate an African American theatre culture, the need for greater funding of African American theatres, and the need for African Americans artists to focus their efforts on African American culture rather than White American artistry. Brustein's direct response submitted to the Theatre Communication in an October 1996 article titled, "Subsidized Racism," expressing his opposition to Wilson's stance, led to much critical reaction from both cultural sides, and subsequently, to the Town Hall Debate in 1997 which became an extended dialogue about color blind casting. As with the NTCP's 1986 symposium, theatre practitioners from many cultural backgrounds participated in the discourse, however, the forum focused primarily on the idea of an exclusively African American theatre (represented by Wilson) and White America's rejoinder (represented by Brustein). In this new millennium, more than a full decade following the 1997 debate, the polarized views are further apart than ever as artists on both sides of the issue struggle to fashion a present and future position for color blind casting in theatre arts.

Color blind casting, as a sub-category of non-traditional casting, carries different meaning for different practitioners. The inarguable designation is inherent in the term – blindness to color and/or race in the casting of theatrical roles. Color and race are not necessarily the same, however, they are often regarded as such. According to Webster's New World Dictionary, color, in regards to ethnicity means "the color of one's skin" whereas race is defined as "any group of people having the same ancestry . . . having the same activities, habits, ideas, etc. . . ." (289, 1197). Color refers to an external physical feature and race refers to lineage and customs. The term "color blindness" is not without its limitations. At this stage in society, however, it is the term that is familiarly employed by many so it will be used throughout this writing.

Assessing color blind casting in theatre -- its history and the ongoing controversy that surrounds it -- and offering a proposal for its appropriate use is most relevant in an emerging polycultural era. Political scientist Robert C. Lieberman states, "Race -- particularly the color line dividing white from black . . . has always been central to American political life" (1). The division has also become a central focus in theatre. Color blind casting has been seen as such -- an African American and White American struggle -- by the American public and clearly needs resolution from these standpoints. Other cultural groups participated in the national forum of 1986 and in the 1997 debate on color blind and non-traditional theatre practices, yet the focus consistently remained centered on African American/White American concerns. Thus, the discussion will be taken up from these two generally opposing positions. In the last twenty-five years resistance to color blind casting has arisen from African Americans primarily while White Americans, at least in theory, have overwhelmingly been in support of color blind practices. Certainly there are issues regarding color blind practices to be addressed by other cultural groups. This is, by no means, an exhaustive investigation as other racial groups in America have vital perspectives that are associated with this issue, as well. William Sun, Jennifer L. Sheppard, Jacqueline Lo, and Angela C. Pao have discussed color blind practices in light of Asian American views and Antonio Campo-Guzman has written about color blind casting from a

Latino perspective. Every ethnic group deserves a full historical and socio-political treatment regarding non-traditional theatre and color blind casting. Although such a study would be a worthwhile endeavor, the scope of this work cannot cover the full complexities of multi-racial views and relationships to color blind casting. Thus, this study must necessarily be limited.

By the close of the 20th century, following the explosive, emotional 1997 August Wilson-Robert Brustein Town Hall Debate, dialogue about color blind theatre died away. Artists and theatre professionals entrenched themselves in scholarship, writing analyses of color blind casting in performance theory, particularly in relationship to the classics and classical periods. After the year 2000 literary offerings on color blind practices in theatre have included Rodney K. Douglas' *The Concept and Practice of Mixed Race Casting in New York Theatres and Other Regions* (2002), Arthur Knight's *Disintegrating the Musical: Black Performance and American Musical Film* (2002), Sean Griffin's "The Gang's All Here: Generic versus Racial Integration in the 1940s Musical" (2002), Ayanna Thompson's "Practicing a Theory/Theorizing a Practice: An Introduction to Shakespearean Colorblind Casting" (2006), and Margo Hendricks' "Visions of Color: Spectacle, Spectators, and the Performance of Race" (2006). Open dialogue and debate about color blind casting fell away in American theatre society. In a 2005 interview for the *African American Review* N. Graham Nesmith posed the question about his position on non-traditional casting to director Lloyd Richards. Richards succinctly responded, " each generation has to come to terms with its non-traditional casting and settle it. I have been involved with non-traditional casting since the time I was in college. I do not go around that circle any more."

Theatre professionals had begun pulling away from investigative public discussions about race and politics, non-traditional theatre, and color blind practices since the 1990s. Certainly, much has been written about color blind *practices* and non-traditional theatre. But little, aside from Douglas' 2002 treatment of mixed race casting, has been written of late about the highly emotional socio-psychological aspects of color blind theory. For example, Thompson's *Colorblind Shakespeare* is reportage -- a collection of scholarly essays on performance theory. Helen Gilbert and Jacqueline Lo's 2002 comprehensive treatment of cross-cultural theatre is a matrix for using non-traditional theatre practices. Jennifer L. Sheppard's essay "Theatrical Casting–Discrimination or Artistic Freedom (1991)" examines color blind casting practices from a legal standpoint. In "Power and Problems of Performance across Ethnic Lines," William Sun states the aim of his 2000 article as an "anthropological perspective as it relates to education; aesthetics in relation to professional theatre; and a political perspective in relation to unemployment" (88). Socio-psychological implications are rarely, if at all, mentioned in recent works about color blind and non-traditional theatre practices. This is not to say that varied responses about the practice have not been offered.

Every time a major color blind casting production is launched, such as the casting of Phylicia Rashad in "August: Osage County," the public and the theatre population cast vehement votes in favor of or against the artistic choices in endless blogs and newspaper editorials.

Nesmith quoted Lloyd Richards as saying, "The theatre, in its own way, has been one of the most forward thinking places relative to race." However, other fields of study have been leading the way toward addressing the issues. The social and political sciences and the field of education have been rigorously investigating color blind theory and practice and its impact on society at large. Darrell Cleveland edited *A Long Way to Go: Conversations about Race by African American Faculty and Graduate Students* in 2004, which addressed color blind policies as racist practice in higher education throughout the 22 chapters. Lieberman published *Shaping Race Policy* in 2005 about color blind theories and their racist implications in public policy-making arenas such as housing administration, social security, employment, and the penal system. A group of seven sociologists collaborated that same year on a book titled *Whitewashing Race: The Myth of a Color-Blind Society* (University of California Press). These studies are not the first regarding social, legal, and other policy-making issues surrounding race in American society. The Carnegie Commission funded a collaborative study in 1944 to examine the incorporation of minorities into American life and the idea of a more color blind society. Post Emancipation laws, particularly during the enactment of the Fourteenth Amendment in 1866 instigated a great deal of discussion about color blind constitutionalism although the term 'color blind' does not appear in the wording of that legislature. Studies centering on these issues have been conducted periodically over the past century but they do not match the explosion of writing in the social sciences that has been produced specifically about color blind theories in the past two decades.

As the social sciences lead the way, the theatre environ can model its approach to group social needs in an effort to more reliably weigh out future directions for the positioning of color blind theatre in theory and practice. What is needed in the 21st century is a systematic scholarly exploration of the construct of the practice of color blind casting, why it is constructed, and how and why it might or might not be useful. From a socio-psychological perspective, examining how the placement and use of color blind theatre affects the needs of its participants differs from other treatments of color blindness in theatre and society. Employing this methodology can present a solid and hopefully, indisputable premise for affording African Americans greater consideration in the issue of color blind practices.

By first extricating color blind casting from other forms of non-traditional theatre a working definition can be established prior to fashioning a viable model for practice. Then the groundwork of the argument, providing various personal perspectives, and a birdseye view of the impasse with which we, as Americans, are faced can be laid. Personal perspectives from various directors, producers, writers, journalists, sociologists, actors, and historians are not offered to provide a survey of pro- and anti-color blind sentiments. Each personal perspective elucidates a specific point about the intricate aspects of the issue that factor into the cultural and artistic gridlock we are currently facing. The examination reveals the broader issues surrounding color blind casting for its participants and sets forth the task of understanding a balancing of the needs of both African Americans and White Americans in light of the issue.

In presenting African American views on color blind casting, an African American particularist agenda, which will be discussed through sociologist Tommie Shelby's definition, is not proffered . The platform is presented to demonstrate its similarities to separatism -- an accusation that has been leveled at African Americans who are in favor of African American theatre practices over color blind theatre practices – in an effort to shed light on the artistic concerns of African Americans and to demystify the notion of racial conflict as a basis of these concerns. In presenting the views of White Americans views it is hoped that the analysis is not perceived as an indictment but as an illumination of the position of White American artists and practitioners in the great race debate that has become contemporary theatre's manacle. As society evolves in the upcoming decades we will undoubtedly need to continue to assess and reassess the theories and practices of color blind casting in theatre. It is my hope that the analyses and subsequent prescriptions herein will serve as a springboard for positioning color blind practices in theatre and society.

13

Chapter One

COLOR BLIND CASTING AND NON-TRADITIONAL THEATRE

The American theatre has never really known what to do with its Black performers – Jack Kroll

Identifying and outlining non-traditional practices in theatre is a preface to distinguishing the various types of non-traditional casting, including color blind casting, which comes under its umbrella term. The purpose of such careful demarcations is two-fold: a) to clarify the current definitional confusions and blurred perceptions that have caused much nonproductive contention among theatre participants around the world; b) to trace the evolved meaning and view of non-traditional casting practices in society as a whole. The ultimate purpose is to gain a practical perspective and approach to analyzing color blind casting's value and place in non-traditional casting.

In *Beyond Tradition*, Harry Newman, co-founder and executive director of the non-profit organization The Non-Traditional Casting Project (NTCP) and Clinton Turner Davis classify non-traditional casting in theatre as ". . . the casting of ethnic, female or disabled actors in roles where race, ethnicity, gender or physical capability are not necessary to the characters' or play's development" (Davis, Newman, Introduction). Newman and Davis go on to splinter the broad concept of non-traditional casting into four distinct categories: a) Societal Casting; b) Cross-cultural Casting; c) Conceptual Casting; and d) Blind Casting. Producer and director Rodney K. Douglas used Newman's definition and its sub-categories in his 2001 dissertation on the subject, adding the terms "interracial," "cross-over," and "mixed-race" casting to the mix (1-2). Angela C. Pao uses Harry Newman's and the Non-Traditional Casting Project's definition as the basis of her analysis in her November 2000 essay "Recasting Race: Casting Practices and Racial Formations" (2). William H. Sun lays out a very convincing argument for the prescriptive use of non-traditional casting practices based, again on Harry Newman's designations (87).

15

Jennifer L. Sheppard also relies on Newman's definition in her discussion of the legislative aspects of non-traditional casting (282-283). Across the board, the NTCP's definition has been widely accepted. In referring to non-traditional theatre, I mean non-traditional casting of traditional drama and drama where the non-traditional elements are written in.

What has become known as traditional casting in theatre was once, in the truest sense, non-traditional in that roles meant for cultural minorities and women were assigned to non-minorities and men. The convention can be found since the inception of formal theatre during the ancient Greek period when men and boys played the roles of women and Greeks played the roles of cultural others, as in *The Persians* by Aeschylus. Non-traditional casting continued to be the norm in legitimate venues throughout the Roman, Medieval, Renaissance, and the Elizabethan/Jacobean periods with a few exceptions. Japanese theatre included female performers like Shinto priestess Okuni of Izumo in the early 17th century. In England during the Medieval, Renaissance, and Elizabethan/Jacobean periods more traditional theatre transpired in small, traveling (often family) troupes that performed for royalty and chance audiences throughout the countryside, and non-licensed companies which, " . . . not under royal patronage or that of other noblemen as members of an officially allowed company, e.g. the King's Men (under Elizabeth, the Lord Chamberlain's Men), the Admiral's Men, Queen Anne's Men, etc, were always in danger of the Statute of 1572 (and its successors), which declared them to be rogues and vagabonds punishable by law" (Evans 92). Women were not allowed on the English Stage. Sixteenth century playwright Thomas Nashe wrote in 1592:

> Our players are not as the players beyond sea, a sort of
> squirming, bawdy comedians, that have whores and
> common courtesans to play women's parts and forbear no
> immodest speech or unchaste action that may procure
> laughter; but our scene is more stately furnished than ever
> it was in the time of Roscius, our representations
> honourable and full of gallant resolution, not consisting,
> like theirs, of a pantaloon, a whore, and a zany . . . (Evans
> 92-93)

Nashe is referring to commedia dell'arte, the popular theatrical form of the Italian renaissance. Traveling commedia troupes generally employed seven men and three women. Another more traditional practice occurred during the Spanish Golden Age when Spanish acting troupes included women—a practice that grew out of the Middle Ages when women were permitted to act in religious dramas throughout continental Europe, excluding England. The Spanish attempted to ban women from the stage throughout the 16th century until 1587 when women were legally allowed to perform. In 1596 a new ban was reinstated until 1599 when only wives and daughters of company members could lawfully perform.

Non-traditional casting practices, namely the use of men in women's roles continued throughout Europe and England until the French Neoclassical period of the mid 17th century when women became members of the French acting companies. Madeleine Bèjart helped found the Théâtre Illustre, along with Molière and other actors. Molière's young wife Armande Béjart, the daughter of Madeleine Bèjart, performed in many of her husband's plays. The Comèdie Francaise, established in 1680, included actress Ëlisa Fèlix and later in the late 19th century, actress Sarah Bernhardt. Women playing women's roles in the traditional manner became considerably more common in colonial America. One of the earliest acting troupes arriving from England in 1751 was the Lewis Hallam company which included actor Lewis Hallam, Sr., his actress wife, their three children, and seven additional actors.

Gender-based non-traditional theatre in early America proliferated as actresses like Lydia Thompson in the role of Robinson Crusoe and Lotta Crabtree in the role of a drummer boy elected to play male/boy roles. Race-based non-traditional theatre in early America remained consistent and intact until the early 20th century with Edmund Kean playing Othello, Mrs. George C. Howard playing Topsy in *Uncle Tom's Cabin*, and White performers in Africanface doing minstrel shows.

Throughout recorded dramatic history, society has witnessed far more non-traditional casting than traditional casting. With the onset of realism in modern drama, traditional casting became the norm for White Americans by the early 20th century in mainstream theatre. At that time blackface makeup was abandoned (but prevailed in film until the mid 20th century) and men played men's roles while non-traditional casting was still in effect for African Americans playing roles in dramas written by White Americans. The convention of African Americans engaged in non-traditional casting practices formally began with The African Company in 1821 when African American actors performed classics like *Richard III* and continued through the present. African American performers also donned blackface makeup in an inverted type of non-traditional performance with African Americans imitating Whites who were imitating African Americans until the early 20th century when the practice was finally abandoned by comic greats like Bert Williams and George Walker. The use of blackface was criticized and rejected by African Americans as early as the last quarter of the 19th century with concerted efforts being made to create non-minstrelsy roles and shows for African Americans. African American musicals and straight dramas proliferated in the last decade of that century. *The Octoroons*, written in 1895 by John W. Isham, was one of the first musicals to break with minstrelsy conventions. Isham followed up that effort with *Oriental America* which did not use the customary minstrel cakewalk (traditional walkaround) but ended with an operatic medley.

Great strides toward establishing a more self-defined African American theatre aesthetic were being made by writers, producers, and performers like Isham, Bob Cole, William Marion Cook, Joseph Cotter, Ernest Hogan, and renowned poet Paul Lawrence Dunbar, who co-wrote *Clorindy* in 1898. Despite the fact that Bert Williams and George Walker were still performing on Broadway in blackface as late as 1903, they were also participating in the rash of new musicals and plays during what has been called the golden age of the Negro in theatre. African American companies sprang up in Harlem, including the Crescent Theatre and the Lafayette Players, which preceeded the birth of the Harlem Renaissance in 1921. Williams' and Walker's involvement in productions that utilized blackface makeup were seemingly born out of reluctance. According to Loften Mitchell, "The tall, proud, literate West Indian did not look like White Americans thought Negroes should. And so, despite his objections, he was compelled to wear burnt cork, to darken his face, and shuffle like a so-called 'darky'" (Voices 25). In Mitchell's view Williams and Walker were oppressed heroes:

Negro pioneers—Williams and Walker, Cole and Johnson and others—stepped in to revolutionize theatrical concepts regarding the Negro. But they fought their revolution on the grounds of the oppressors. They used the same weapons—the blackface, the low comedy—and did the things whites would pay to see Negroes do. They used for their reasoning the belief that whites would not accept them any other way. These Negroes, then, were true to the first American Revolution. They engaged in a reform movement, not a revolution. They fought a defensive action, rather than an offensive one. The wrecking of the African Company, therefore, reached down through the years from 1821 and reverberated into the 1920s and beyond. (*Black Drama* 84)

Mitchell does not clearly establish a connection between White, mainstream acceptance of African American performers in White roles/African American roles created by Whites and the reform of White (or African American for that matter) concepts regarding African Americans. What is clear is the idea that African American artists were seeking an ideological change in how they represent their identities on the American stage. Mitchell's comparison to the first American Revolution to the pioneering efforts of Williams, Walker, Cole, et al, however, is inappropriate in that America had used revolutionary dissimilation measures in the late 18th century to effect reform while Williams and other early African American entertainers used assimilation to effect reform.

Today, when we speak of traditional theatre and traditional casting practices we are referring to what has occurred in the past, rather than what is accurate and appropriate. Traditional theatre practices in America, or the theatre of the past 350 years, had inherent boundaries that designated roles based on societal expectations and this is still true today. Non-traditional theatre of today offers a way out of the limitations of societal expectations and mandates. Practitioners of non-traditional theatre have employed this type of theatre for a myriad of purposes—conscious and unconscious—articulated and inexpressible. Actor's Equity Association's espousal of non-traditional theatre practices in the mid 1980s was meant to establish a foundation of equal opportunity employment. The union's policy-making move was further developed into outreach efforts for artistic ethics and social education by Harry Newman and the efforts of the Non-Traditional Casting Project. Newman and his supporters developed the concept of non-traditional casting beyond a mere employment clause and into a usable tool through careful categorization. The NTCP splintered the broad category of non-traditional casting, subsuming cross-cultural, blind, societal, and conceptual casting under its banner. The purpose in defining and illustrating the various classifications is to ultimately extricate the term "color-blind casting" from the mass, refine its meaning and implications if necessary, and to establish a succinct working model upon which to base the premise of this study.

The NTCP's widely accepted sub-categories of non-traditional casting are:

Societal Casting: Ethnic, female or disabled actors are cast in roles they perform in society as a whole

Cross-cultural Casting: the entire world of a play is translated to a different cultural setting

Conceptual Casting: an ethnic, female or disabled actor is cast in a role to give a play greater resonance

Blind Casting: all actors are cast without regard to their race, ethnicity, gender or physical capability

*Color blind casting is a subcategory of Blind casting

Each of the above sub-categories have been used singularly and collectively in conscious, and often self-conscious, attempts to explore new creative avenues, to unearth further insights from particular works, to provide increased employment opportunities, and to address the problem of under-representation of minority groups.

The key task in determining the placement of color blind casting in American theatre is mapping out the scope of its actual meaning in light of other types of non-traditional casting practices. First, societal casting, where ethnic, female, or disabled actors are cast in roles they perform in society as a whole, in its most ideal form, is essentially traditional casting given its conformity to society but it is also non-traditional in that it goes against the grain of what has occurred in the past. In a perfect world, societal casting would not be included under non-traditional casting. One example of societal casting was a 1990 production of *Line* by Israel Horowitz at the University of Missouri where this writer cast an African American male and an interracial couple (East Indian male and White American female) with the intent of establishing a realistic world. The drama's plot of five characters struggling to attain and maintain first position in a line for admittance to an unknown event lends itself to cultural pluralism due to its universal thematic scheme. The additional intent of the casting choices in this production was to demonstrate a particular idealism in portraying the commonality of life goals among various racial groups. The casting choices were distinctly in keeping with societal casting practices but differed from color blind casting in its intent.

Conceptual casting whereby an ethnic, female or disabled actor is cast in a role to give a play greater resonance, most lends itself to underscoring thematic intention. To place African American actress Gloria Foster in the role of Medea might emphasize the cultural separation that existed between the main character and the world of her husband, Jason. The New York Shakespeare Festival's 1964 production of *Antony and Cleopatra* is another example of conceptual casting. Half of the 20 member touring company was to be African American and the production was billed as a celebration of racial harmony to commemorate the 400th anniversary of Shakespeare's birth (Pao 9). The production would fall under the category of conceptual casting because it used African American actors for greater social resonance.

Cross-cultural casting, according to the NTCP's definition, is perhaps the most easily accepted of non-traditional theatre practices and is also the practice that is often confusingly called color blind casting. It is found acceptable because it provides a glimpse into another cultural view without the semiological confusion of the other categories. Cross-cultural casting lifts the story out of the playwright's original world, depositing the story into a different cultural setting. There are clear-cut cases of this type of production, notably, Ntozake Shange's 1980 adaptation of Bertolt Brecht's *Mother Courage* at the Public Theatre in New York. Shange exchanged the Swedish war and a Swedish woman and her children for the Civil War with an African American woman and her children. The script was, for the most part, Brecht's script with factual changes. Other examples are *Gospel at Colonus* based upon *King Lear* and set in a Baptist church and the WPA's version of *Macbeth* by the Negro Unit of the Federal Theatre Project, under African American actress and director Rose McClendon, and White American producer John Houseman. In that experimental time of the depression, providing work for Americans was the aim and theatre became the vehicle for many artists to push boundaries with the classics. *Macbeth* was set in Haiti with an all African American cast under the direction of Orson Welles. Part of the rationale for the setting was the similarity between the life of the character Macbeth and the life of the historic Haitian army officer, Christophe. Further supporting the rationale for the Haitian context was the easy transition of the three witches from Shakespeare's original into Voodoo priestesses. According to Houseman the cross-cultural play concept was well received:

> The production was a great success. It was much admired uptown and downtown. It actually played on Broadway for four months and then toured, and strange as it may seem went all the way to the Dallas World's Fair. (Davis and Newman 13)

Not all productions of the classics that use an all-African American cast can be considered authentic cross-cultural casting by the NTCP's definition, however. A great number of productions of the past and present using all-African American or predominantly African American casts have merely substituted African American actors for an all-White cast without transporting the story into an African American setting. Examples include the earliest extant all-African American production of Shakespeare's *Richard III* by the African Grove Theatre Company in 1821, Circle in the Square's 1967 production of *A Midsummer Night's Dream*, and many of the classics produced by Joseph Papp at the New York Public Theatre such as Eugene O'Neill's *A Long Day's Journey into Night* in 1971 and *The Cherry Orchard* (1973).

Joseph Papp, as a pioneer in non-traditional casting, "/ theater to represent the ethnically diverse city that surroun his youth on Manhattan's Lower East Side" (Simonson 85 to his style of casting the classics as "interracial casting" (Simonson ⁁ᴗ⁏. This holds true for his Mobile Theatre Units of African American and Latino actors that presented Shakespeare in underprivileged African American and Latino communities throughout New York City and his productions at the Public Theatre. But many of his productions were neither societal, cross-cultural, or color-blind. They were merely dramas written by Whites and cast with African Americans and Latinos. Clive Barnes of the New York Times wrote in his review of *The Cherry Orchard*, "Mr. Papp felt the need to develop a concept of a classical theater for black actors. At this stage in black nationalism in our political development, Mr. Papp believes less and less in integrated casts" (Simonson 81). Likewise, the Denver Center Theatre Company's 2004 production of *A Streetcar Named Desire* with an all-African American cast did not fall into any of the above categories. It was simply reverse race casting. Many plays of this ilk are labeled color blind.

Blind casting, of all the categories of non-traditional casting is the greatest anomaly and possibly the least purely realizable as a practical venture in theatre. Angela Pao asserts, "Among the various types of non-traditional casting, colorblind casting – like the model of a colorblind society it is supposed to exemplify –has been seen at once as the most idealistic and the most pernicious form" (4). According to the NTCP this particular practice attempts to ignore ethnicity, gender, and physical capability in casting dramatic roles (unless they are germane to the play's purpose) and aims to compel audiences to disregard the demographics, as well. The 1990 Broadway show *Miss Saigon* is an example of a color blind casting situation in that English actor Jonathan Pryce was cast in the starring (Asian) role. This is one of the few cases of reverse color blind casting in the past 20 years (outside of television and film). Blind casting creates the possibilities for conceptual and societal casting practices and provides the imagination for cross-cultural casting. In this work, color blind casting is the focal point. Not all practitioners agree upon the meaning or usage of color blind casting, let alone understand how to apply it onstage. Joseph Papp stated, "I was thinking of ways to eliminate color a factor in casting, but be on the other hand . . . very aware of color on the stage" (Simonson 85). Libby Appel, artistic director of the Oregon Shakespeare Festival claims, "There is no such thing as colorblindness. When people look at the stage they see the colors of the actors" (Pao 15). Peter Erickson states, "In the narrow theatrical sense, it [color blind] means placing actors of color in the roles of white characters and thus disrupting the strict racial alignment of actor with character" (Thompson 241). Many have grappled with the elusive meaning and application of the term as well as the inherent contradictions of being simultaneously ignorant and conscious of race. In trying to pin the practice down to a single definition we get further entangled in its meaning. Vit Wagner of the Toronto Star simplified matters in his definition based on a continuum. At one end of his spectrum lies "soft color blindness" that he says, "At minimum, color-blind casting means allowing non-white actors to play characters not specifically written down as black or Asian – an innocuous, inclusionary gesture. . . ." and on the other end is what Wagner explains as, "At maximum, it means a completely color-blind approach, even to the point of having, say, black and white actors play twins . . . "("Wouldn't She Make"). The difference between the two ends of Wagner's continuum lies in the practitioner's intentions to be either color conscious or color blind. Ralph Berry agrees, stating, "There are now two kinds of casting conventions on the stage, 'colour-blind' and 'colour-conscious.'" (35). Early efforts of the NTCP were primarily color conscious.

The NTCP made every effort to center the 1986 first national symposium around the concept of non-traditional casting without highlighting the issues in terms of specific racial divisions. Few direct mentions were made to color blindness and the event included diverse participants such as Rene Buch, artistic director of Repertorio Español, Tisa Chang, artistic director of Pan Asian Repertory Theatre, Maria Irene Fornes, playwright and director, and Rudy Martin of the American Indian Community House. Yet, much of the dialogue became centered on African American and White American positioning as seen in the following excerpts:

> When we talk about non-traditional casting, I hope we are not talking about doing all black plays or all white plays. Integrating black and white together, I think, is more interesting – Fran Weissler, Producer (Davis and Newman 21)

I must strongly dissent with the [idea] that an audience wasn't ready to see James Earl Jones play Iago – John Dillon, Artistic Director, Milwaukee Repertory Theatre (Davis and Newman 39)

We're doing a production in the American Repertory Theatre of THE END OF THE WORLD. The point is not parts that I knew could be played by people, [but] that was a part that I said, "No, you cannot have a black person because no black person would be at the rank." That isn't the issue of that scene and one would get right beyond that scene, that aspect of it – Arthur Kopit, Playwright (Davis and Newman 41)

We're talking about color-blind casting. In this culture it's very difficult to avoid color-wise casting. We are so sensitive to these issues even in a negative sense that any kind of casting that is done has certain resonances through the culture. We see Trofimov playing that role in the CHERRY ORCHARD and we hear about the serfs and then we immediately see a black actor, we liken the serfs to American blacks and it sets up a whole chain of associations. Can we talk, in this society, about color-blind casting? – Elinor Fuchs, Theatre Critic, Dramaturg, Educator (Davis and Newman 44)

I remember a few years back in Washington, DC, watching James Earl Jones in OF MICE AND MEN. Now, if you know the play, you know there is a scene with Crooks and why Crooks, the black man, is not allowed in the bunkhouse. Therefore James Earl Jones' presence as Lenny didn't make sense. It didn't seem to impinge on ticket sales one iota –John Dillon, Artistic Director, Milwaukee Repertory Theatre (Davis and Newman 48)

In our city, you couldn't convince the press to do a story
that you are doing a show casting things against race. We
have taken things a step further. A show like AIN'T
MISBEHAVIN' we did, once again, when we were low in
the coffers with a multi-racial cast. We have done FOR
COLORED GIRLS . . . without an all black cast – Jack
Reuler, Artistic Director, Mixed Blood Theatre (Davis and
Newman 73)

The implication of these statements and many other observations made
by participants at the symposium is that the notion of non-traditional
theatre tends to stir up images of African American/White American
relations. Discussions about Asian, Native American, Latino, Jewish, the
physically disabled, and women in blind casting took a back seat to
discussions about African American inclusion onstage even while mostly
avoiding the term "color blind." Furthermore, there was very little mention
of societal, cross-cultural, or conceptual casting. Blind casting, specifically
color blind casting, resonated deeply in the minds of producers,
playwrights, directors, historians, sociologists, critics, and humanitarians
alike, as the basis of non-traditional theatre even though it was rarely
mentioned. It was, in fact, August Wilson's attachment to the term "color
blind" in 1996 that brought the public into a direct and contentious debate
about its merits. Wilson was an artist not a scholar, which created a degree
of confusion and abstractness around his argumentation. He was, in
actuality, referring to all forms of non-traditional theatre that placed
African American actors in non-African America dramatic contexts.
    There is some truth to Appel's assertion that there is no such thing as
color blindness from the audience's point of view. The semiotics of theatre
demands recognition of what is seen onstage and a processing of assigned
meaning to the experience. From a director's or producer's standpoint,
Papp's intentions may be difficult to achieve. Here, the blindness is a
mental endeavor rather than a physical feat of not seeing what the eye
beholds unless a director or producer literally avoids visual contact with
the actor. The action would not ensure a true blindness because actors in
professional theatre are selected on the basis of reputation with
foreknowledge of appearance or on the basis of submitted headshots. So,

blindness in casting is essentially an impossibility. Given these parameters, the question still remains. Is blind casting a practice that supports African American theatre or detracts from the ultimate aims of African American society in the realm of theatre? Answering this question is the central aim of this thesis.

Robert Brustein, director and scholar, who situated himself against Wilson in the Town Hall debate of 1997, would say that decisions about the appropriateness of color blind casting should come from society as a whole in a universal effort to map the course of American theatre practices and the progress of American society, as a whole. He is correct in determining that color blind casting is a practice that involves many. There are writers, directors, actors, and audience to consider. It is safe and accurate to say that the end result of such casting impacts participants cross-culturally. It is also realistic to say that color blind casting can be a useful, innovative technique for expanding the creative and social horizons of society. However, like the amazing medical discovery of penicillin, there are side effects that must be considered for long- range effectiveness. The considerations should rightfully be in the hands of all parties who will ultimately experience the long-range effects on its social system. White American society will, undoubtedly, be impacted by the opportunity to work with cultural others and experience non-traditional art as will African Americans by the opportunity to work with different art forms and other cultural outlooks. Therefore, other cultures notwithstanding, the decision lies, to one degree or another, between the groups. This simple equation should not negate the perspectives and concerns of other cultural groups regarding color blind practices. It merely picks up the argument where Wilson and Brustein left off – The theatre world's positioning around the concept and creation of color blind casting.

For better or for worse, the main players in this exchange on non-traditional, blind casting have become African Americans and White Americans, which raises the question, "How has the topic evolved for both groups?" The first formal use of color blind casting occurred in 1952 with the Greenwich Mews Theatre which "insisted that its policy was to cast without regard for color unless the play specifically called for Negro or white characters" (Mitchell *African Drama* 158). While the now familiar debate ensued about the intrinsic worth of such policy, little has been officially recorded concerning the opposing views at that time. Historian Mitchell, remembers the prevailing sentiments as such:

It was a policy that created a lot of "pros" and "cons." The pros declared this was part of the battle – of a people working at a given craft without racial barriers. Actors, they argued, should not be kept from playing roles because of color. Jewish actors play Italian roles and Irish actors play Germans. Why then exclude the Negro actor from this opportunity? The cons were equally pointed. This, they said, was not the question at all. They were being falsely integrated, and the result of this would be deculturization and dehumanization of Negroes. The answer, they claimed, was to put on more plays by and about Black people. (*Black Drama* 158-159)

It is not difficult to ascertain which position was primarily held by African American artists. Overwhelmingly, critical response from African American directors, actors, producers, sociologists, museum curators, and historians, at the NCTP's Symposium and following the Wilson-Brustein debate expressed a range of concern regarding nontraditional and color blind casting, from conditional cautiousness to adamant opposition. Early recorded views tended toward mixed acceptance with an assertion of cultural concern during the mid to late 1980s as evidenced in the following passages:

. . . The play is always the thing. If you have an appearance of say a mixed race family on stage where the author did not account for it, that [raises] a very sensitive issue for a lot of people. I am not worried about the sensitivity. I am worried about [the audience] getting over the hurdle of that, if it is a hurdle for them, and going on with the play. If it stops the play, I think it is something you have to deal with – James Earl Jones, Actor (Davis and Newman 77).

. . . American theatre, mainstream theatre, is essentially white theatre. We live in a society that has had a racist history and [is] at best a race conscious society. Consequently, what is reflected on the stage has been limited to that particular attitude. When a theatre does not reflect the reality of the society of the people in it, it is going to lack those voices, that energy. . . . Around the country, particularly in universities, [presentations of] the classics should not be based on racial casting. As I tell universities, Shakespeare did not write about white people. . . . There has to be an inclusion – a wider inclusion, first and foremost of black material in which the presence of black people will be a natural part of the artistic project. Then you can start to talk about everything else – Douglas Turner Ward, Artistic Director, Negro Ensemble Company (Davis and Newman 19).

I must blame the directors and producers. I don't think it's necessarily the audience. The plays I've seen the A.R.T. (American Repertory Theatre) produce which are not embedded culturally, which do not require this kind of actor because they are essentially domestic dramas have been quite successful. It is partly the audience and the nature of theatre, but I think that can change as other things in America have changed. The burden rests essentially on the producers and directors who select plays which will allow a greater participation of the audience with an actor who happens to be black. But, by choosing plays which are class and culturally embedded they make that difficult for the audience – Orlando Patterson, Professor of Sociology, Harvard University (Davis and Newman 25).

We [La Mama] are not a traditional theatre. We strive not to do the so-called traditional play. . . . I personally don't believe that a Philadelphia Biddle should be cast as anything but that WASP person that the Philadelphia Biddle is. I think that plays and theatres and staging should be created to embrace a whole. I don't particularly believe at all that THE PHILADELPHIA STORY should be presented with me, Ellen Stewart, playing the Biddle. I cannot see that. So as usual, I make the appeal that with this so-called "mainstream" [theatre], why don't all of us make a concerted effort to try to educate the mainstream by giving them something beyond the so-called PHILADELPHIA STORY in which only the white WASP person should be there – Ellen Stewart, Artistic Director, La Mama Theatre Company (Davis and Newman 23).

One common concern was the paucity of material that hindered fair representation of African Americans. In this instance, the term "fair" is used both quantitatively and qualitatively – fair in numbers and fair in depiction. Additionally, commentaries put the onus for preserving African American theatrical art upon the shoulders of producers, directors, and playwrights in a bid for greater selections outside of mainstream American theatre.

In 1997 the *American Theatre Journal* invited written commentary from a number of the Town Hall Debate participants about the issues that were raised. African American participant feedback was consistent with earlier views:

Since I haven't yet found anything colorblind about the way America views her children (or her guests), I have a difficult time accepting the principle of color-blindness in theatrical casting – unless it is done in sync with programming that illuminates and celebrates cultural and ethnic distinction as well. The circumstance in which we find ourselves, however, is not just simply about color (though not being able to effectively get to that subject is most distracting!). It's about an arrogance that is very American and an ill-preparedness when it comes to being able to deal with the cultural and aesthetic baggage of others. Couple that with a crippling fear of difference in our midst, and it becomes clear that we've got a lot of serious work to do – Ricardo Khan, Co-Founder and Artistic Director, Crossroads Theatre Company ("On Cultural Power" 15).

Wilson's points ranged wildly and at random from the entirely valid to the invalid and preposterous. . . . In this thicket of indefinites, Brustein's positions were based almost entirely upon a misapprehension of Wilson's points. Brustein took Wilson's references to the black militancy of the 60s and to classifying himself as a "race man" to mean that Wilson was advocating separatism, as in a return to social segregation, and called such thinking a "poisonous racial consciousness." But it doesn't necessarily follow that African American theatre leads to separatism and segregation, which translates into racial hatred and a fascist intent – Michelle Wallace, Author and Cultural Critic ("On Cultural Power" 14, 56).

In theatre, as in life, people speak about equality, race relations and diversity. . . . For me it's not a question of "black" theatre or "white" theatre. It is a question of creating a theatre where all voices can be present and can have a safe space to be heard. . . . We were on the journey when the Lila Wallace-Reader's Digest Fund's Resident

Theatre Initiative stepped forward to provide the positive catalyst we needed for the Alliance and the Atlanta community to come together and re-imagine what theatre in Atlanta can be. The Fund's grant to the Alliance in 1992 allowed us to commission new plays by and about Black Americans, to broaden our audiences for these plays as well as the entire season through marketing and community relations, and to strengthen the diversity of our staff through professional post-graduate internships – Kenny Leon, Artistic Director, Alliance Theatre Company ("On Cultural Power" 61).

We haven't invested in ourselves. I haven't said, "O.K., why don't I sit down and just produce a few weekends of our own theater." I think we should support Black theaters like Woodie King's, but I also think young Black artists of my generation and younger must come together and begin to produce one another's work. And I still want to have access to any theater in the world. I'm classically trained. I am equipped and just as qualified as my white female counterparts to do Shaw, to do Ibsen, to do Shakespeare. Maybe there are times artistically when a particular piece is so specific that it needs to be an all-Eskimo cast. But then there are times when that sensibility of race can be challenged – Lisa Gay Hamilton, Actor (Gold 2).

African American reaction has been consistently outspoken and adamant – African American heritage cannot be replaced onstage with color blind, conceptual, cross-cultural, or societal casting projects, particularly those projects that are originated in non-African American material. In later years, following the Wilson-Brustein debate, emphasis was placed upon the establishment of an African American theatre culture and aesthetic rather than the earlier emphasis on simply creating and selecting African American dramatic material. What has been less consistent is the tone of the inter-cultural argument over the years. In the span of ten years between the NTCP's national symposium and the Town Hall debate between Wilson and Brustein, the direction of the discourse has moved from artistic inclusion to racial contention.

At the NTCP's symposium in 1986, White American participants were generally seeking pragmatic solutions as demonstrated in the following exchange:

> MICHAEL KAHN (Artistic Director, Shakespeare Theatre at the Folger): Perhaps I am changing the subject here, but there is a problem that I perceive that's just happened to me. I wonder if we could address it. I am running a classical theatre and am totally interested in non-traditional casting. I find it embarrassing to be down in Washington, DC, to be talking about minority actors. Yet, when I started asking for actors to appear, a very small minority of the actors who appeared at casting were minority actors. . . .

> ROMULUS LINNEY (Playwright): One of the questions we have been given has something to do with what Michael [Kahn] was trying to say. That question: Ethnic actors suffer a breach of faith in the casting process. How can faith be reinstilled or created. Michael were you saying that minority actors seem to hold back when casting opportunities are presented to them?

> MICHAEL KAHN: That was my experience, yes.

> ROMULUS LINNEY: How can faith be reinstilled or created in the first place? Is it also just a matter of there being too few jobs and of being justifiable reluctant to play stereotypes, caricatures or token roles? Do ethnic actors suffer from a breach of faith? (Davis and Newman 22-23, 26-27)

The symposium had an air of innocence, albeit pained, and inquisitiveness. Participants were interested in conflict resolution. The conflict was in the system and questions arose regarding how to readjust the mechanics of the system to reach a specific goal. The 1997 debate, billed as a discussion ("On Cultural Power: The August Wilson/Robert Brustein Discussion"), was based on very different interests and conflicts. The conflict was embodied in polarized racial stances – primarily African American vs. White American – as represented by Wilson and Brustein. The event held an air of combat as seen in the language of the press' reviews:

> The realities of a complex and culturally diverse society make it difficult to cling to such (pardon the expression) black and white ideals. But for this kind of "crossfire" to be effective, it's essential that the participants take extreme positions for dramatic effect – Terry Byrne, *The Boston Herald*, (Nunns 19).

> The drama of the Wilson-Brustein confrontation lies in their mutual intransigence – Jack Kroll, *Newsweek*, (Nunns, 19).

> There's another reason this ballyhooed bout was so . . . depressing and it has to do with how much Wilson and Brustein's worldview actually have in common: They're both stuck in a monolithic modernism – Alisa Solomon, *The Village Voice*, (Nunns 19).

White American participants in the affair expressed varied sentiments, however, responses indicate a consistent view of the issue as being a polarized race matter between and about African Americans and Whites, more so than an artistic dilemma.

To limit Blacks to Black roles is the kind of restrictive, simplistic, ultimately self-punitive thinking that abnegates not only artistic but also moral imagination: the simple ability to stand in someone else's shoes, obviously essential to theatre, goes to the heart of all ethical thought. And Wilson's prohibitions extend to other ethnic groups and to women, who must not play men's roles, according to him, if that wasn't theauthor's intention – James Leverett, Co-Chair, Department of Dramaturgy and Criticism, Yale School of Drama ("On Cultural Power" 14, 53)

It has always seemed obvious to me that since there are close to 34 million Black-Americans in the United States, with large populations in major cities, there should be a number of theatres led by Black-American directors that express their own cultures, reflect the needs of their communities and, first of all, are self-determining. It may be that reliance is placed on a key leader who is white, as was the case with the Negro Ensemble Company and its managing director in its first years. Or, as with Crossroads Theatre, our only Black LORT theatre, occasionally plays will come from the Western canon and 25 percent or so of the audience will be white. The defining characteristic is that these theatres will be in their own hands, deciding for themselves what they want to produce, what artists they want with them, what they want to become and how to get there. After all, why should Black theatre artists have no other choice but to be guests in other peoples' houses?-- Zelda Fichandler, Artistic Director, Graduate Acting Program, Tisch School of the Arts, New York University ("On Cultural Power" 14, 57)

Once again, we're all compelled to imagine what it must be like to awake every morning to a civic life in which scorn and hostility are going to be as routine a part of the day as morning coffee. He's [Wilson] surely right, also, to step away from the privileges he's earned in order to make a bid for leadership. That said, however, he can't be right about his proposed solution for what amounts to a voluntary apartheid just at the moment of Nelson Mandela's triumph – Gordon Rogoff, Critic and Author ("On Cultural Power" 17)

What can be said of the differences between the two formal gatherings distanced from one another by a decade? Clearly, the purposes had shifted dramatically within that span of time. The nature of the Wilson-Brustein event was a debate which, in and of itself, is confrontational with antagonistic connotations, while the symposium was intended to be a supportive meeting of the minds. Participants came to the debate anticipating a battle and an eventual victor. Stephen Nunns described the night as a sporting event:

The rowdy scene outside the 1,500 seat Town Hall before the event reflected those antagonistic expectations: A wildly diverse combination of theatre folk, intellectuals, celebrities and information-hungry New Yorkers pushed and elbowed ticker scalpers, the media paparazzi, leafleting members of the Revolutionary Workers Party and each other in order to get tickets. . . . If the participants were generally civil in their critiques, the at-times unruly audience was aching for something a little more rowdy. Heckling was *de rigueur* when Wilson was skeptical regarding whether a person of color should perform in *The Cherry Orchard* ("I wouldn't suggest it," he said), an audience member yelled "Fascist!" When Brustein, explaining his critique of *Bring in 'Da Noise, Bring in 'Da Funk*, waxed nostalgic for a community of dancers that didn't acknowledge race ("like the community of Bill Robinson dancing with Shirley Temple"), he elicited groans and hisses from the crowd. A voice that piped up "Maybe we should go back to wearing masks," received a hearty round of applause. (17)

The Town Hall debate was a continuation of the literary debate that Brustein began with his critical response to August Wilson's June 1996 keynote address to the Theatre Communications Group Conference. His address was transcribed the following September into an article titled "The Ground on Which I Stand." Some may say that Wilson invited Brustein into a debate by singling him out for criticism.

> Robert Brustein, writing in an article/review titled "Unity from Diversity" [*The New Republic*, July 19-26,'93] is apparently disturbed that there is a tremendous outpouring of work by "minority artists" which he attributes to cultural diversity. . . . Brustein's surprisingly sophomoric assumption that this tremendous outpouring of work by minority artists leads to confusing standards and that funding agencies have started substituting sociological for aesthetic criteria, leaving aside notions like quality and excellence, shows him to be a victim of 19th-century thinking and the linguistic environment that posits Africans as unqualified. (71)

However, Robert Brustein was not the focus of his address. Wilson stated his focus clearly in the opening statements:

> I have come here today to make a testimony, to talk about the ground on which I stand and all the many grounds on which I and my ancestors have toiled, and the ground of theatre on which my fellow artists and I have labored to bring forth its fruits, its daring and its sometimes lacerating, and often healing truths ("The Ground On Which" 14).

Brustein took exception to Wilson's direct attack by responding in an October *American Theatre* article titled "Subsidized Racism" where he stated his focus as "I frame this reply not just to defend and clarify a personal position which I believe to have been misrepresented but also to debate some of the more troubling general issues raised in his speech" (26). Hence, the face-to-face meeting at Town Hall in January of 1997 became a prolongation of the two artists' views of one another's theatre politics, more so than a discussion of integrating non-traditional casting into American theatre practices, much to the dismay of some participants.

That this event would move us toward a new national synthesis of diversity and multi-culturalism was not likely, given its composition and nature. Anna Deavere Smith, who called it together, is the ultimate fence-sitter, not identified with any racial position or politics by virtue of her scrupulous efforts to represent the entire range of both (a conceptual impossibility). . . . Indeed, I believe the whole matter is ultimately about re-territorializing American culture to fit a dramatic, emerging demographic shift, and that this pseudo event doesn't begin to plumb the depth of the changes that are to come. My interest is in why so many people were so willing to devote so much attention to something that was obviously going to have so little concrete impact – Michele Wallace, Author and Cultural Critic ("On Cultural Power" 56).

In this country, even when it's not about race it's about race. And the second everybody sits down to talk about race it ends up being about everything else but race. And because as a country we're still quite primitive when it comes to negotiating difference, we don't seem to have the skills essential to survive the early steps of any conversation about race. As soon as guilt and rage enter the room, everyone wants to exit. Which means we never get to the real issue - - power: how to share it, relinquish it and learn to live with the awkwardness that comes with change – George C. Wolfe, Producer, New York Shakespeare Festival (Gold 5).

Another significant difference between the two forums on theatre and race was the element of White backlash that resulted. Following the 1997 debate an outpouring of support for Wilson's push for an African American theatre institution was offset by anti-affirmative sentiments:

> Dollars-for-diversity is one reason why working-class whites have all but vanished from the American stage and why so many indifferent Black plays get produced. (Steyn 47).

> Recent years have also brought notable triumphs behind the curtain. *Russell Simmons' Def Poetry Jam* won producer/hip-hop mogul Simmons a Tony award in June. In 2002, Suzan-Lori Parks became the first Black woman to win a Pulitzer Prize for drama. Parks' *Topdog/Underdog* originated at New York's Public Theatre, whose Black artistic director, George C. Wolfe, has overseen celebrated works ranging from the urban musical *Harlem Song* to the Tony-winning Elaine *Stritch at Liberty*. But to hear many of them tell it, Black theater artists continue to face obstacles. (Gardner 1)

Color blind casting and its position in American theatre is not an issue that is completely polarized along race lines. As shown earlier, White American critique has been varied. To a lesser degree, there have been opposing views among African Americans. Rodney K. Douglas favors, what he terms, "mixed race casting."

> One could argue that my perspective on the issue has been influenced by the fact that I am a Black artist. Be that as it may, I have always held a profound belief that mixed racial casting was the proper casting policy, and most in conformity with the concept of theatre, its purpose and its function (vi).

Since the sensitive Town Hall debate of the last decade of 20th century, we are left wondering where America stands on race and theatre and in what directions we are heading. Just after the turn of the 21st century feedback became less specific to theatre but far more abundant in the form of online communications, which is indicative of our changing technological times. Blogs and online journalism, in particular, have become popular forums of expression. An anonymous May 2010 blog posted to the DV Republic website noted that color blind casting in film has lagged behind theatre. Online journalist for the New York Observer, John Heilpern, questioned whether a fuss should be made over color blind casting in the wake of *August: Osage County*, which cast Phylicia Rashad as the White matriarch in 2009. Ronald Fernandez' response in a letter to the New York Times stated, "Let's keep White actresses playing White roles and Blacks playing Black roles."

Full-length theatre books on the topic have been scarce. To date, there has been one published book and two dissertations. Ayanna Thompson published *Colorblind Shakespeare: Performance Theory* in 2006, which is a compilation of essays from various artists dedicated to presenting matrices on how to produce Shakespeare across racial and cultural lines.

As with the previous decade, White American opinions have been varied. More recently the concept of color blindness has been addressed through interdisciplinary and collaborative studies. For example, Charles A. Gallagher contributed his socio-political essay "Color-Blind Privilege: The Social and Political Functions of Erasing the Color Line in Post Race America" to the substantial, multi-discipline volume *Race and Ethnicity in Society: The Changing Landscape*, where he discussed the negative aspects of a color blind society. Brown, Carnoy, Currie, Duster, Oppenheimer, Shultz, and Wellman co- wrote *Whitewashing Race: The Myth of a Color-Blind Society* where the notion of color blindness was unequivocally rejected.

The concluding situation is three-fold: a) the notion of color blindness has taken on a larger dimension in the lives of African Americans; b) the practice of color blindness is one that requires the collaboration of more than one ethnic group; and c) the push toward and the push away from color blind conceptualization are both embroiled in an, as of yet, unresolved conflict. What is equally apparent is the need for resolution as the need for policy-making in theatre and in society at-large presses down upon us.

Chapter Two

ASSESSING NEED FOR COLOR BLIND THEATRE IN SOCIETY

Non-traditional casting is an issue that comes up regularly, on a 10-year cycle. Somehow each generation has to deal with it, and then it fades away and comes up again. . . . Thus, each generation has to come to terms with its non-traditional casting and settle it – Lloyd Richards

To cast color blind or to not cast color blind in theatre productions is a contentious issue that has been volleyed about for more than half a century. The roots of the practice and ensuing deliberations began within African American and White American theatre circles. Varied, often emotional responses from both groups over the past two decades reveals a strong investment in the resolution of the issues raised around color blind casting, which were primarily policy-making issues related to funding and fair hiring practices in the first decade and more philosophical, humanitarian issues in the second decade. At stake for many is the future landscape of society and long-range human relations as well as an abiding concern for the prospects of ethnic theatre in America. Society, beyond the arena of theatre, wants to know what our world will look like in another half century. Will the races have grown apart without sufficient contact to foster awareness, understanding, acceptance, and mutual support, particularly in light of national catastrophes such as the bombing of the Twin Towers in New York on September 11, 2001 or the devastation of Hurricane Katrina in New Orleans in 2005? Others, like August Wilson, worry that the unique cultural expressiveness of their ethnic heritage will lie dormant, undeveloped, underused, and untransferred to later generations, resulting in a loss of cultural identity.

In all cases, the concern is for creating a specific future through the undertaking of specific practices in the present. History has shown us that some form of color blind theatre will always occur along the continuum that defines the broad use of such casting. The practice may be employed to support cultural exclusion as in Elizabethan drama or to support cultural inclusion as in the contemporary thrust toward multiculturalism and fair

41

hiring practices. It may be used for a myriad of reasons between exclusion and inclusion. The fact remains: color blind casting, placing actors in roles against race type is an artistic and logistic prerogative that will always be exercised in one form or another. This has, and will, occur with or without the cooperation of dissidents. As Margo Hendricks states in her article "Gestures of Performance: Rethinking Race in Contemporary Shakespeare," "Despite Wilson's concerns, the issue will not disappear, and such casting decisions remain fraught and much debated" (Thompson 191). We might as well think collaboratively about its function and the best prescription for its use.

The broader macrocosm of society is comprised of many cultural strains that are at once quite distinctive and quite overlapping. To use fabric as an analogy, ideally, each cultural strand would be woven separately and then ultimately conjoined with all other strands to form the "fabric of society." In considering the effects of a practice such as color blind casting that is a broad human concern, influencing and engaging all cultural strands, it becomes necessary to examine the social developmental implications for all strands involved and take into account what is at stake for each. At that point the stakes may be sorted and prioritized for the good of all. The scope of this work has been limited to African American and White American cultural needs in the larger human concern so the examination will begin with a discussion of the social developmental implications for each group. Patricia J. Williams, in *Seeing a Color-Blind Future*, wrote, "While I do want to underscore that I embrace color-blindness as a legitimate hope for the future, I worry that we tend to enshrine the notion with a kind of utopianism whose naïveté will ensure its elusiveness. In the material world ranging from playgrounds to politics, our ideals perhaps need more thoughtful, albeit more complicated, guardianship. By this I mean something more than the 'I think therefore it is' school of idealism. 'I don't think about color, therefore your problems don't exist.' If only it were so easy" (4). It is not so easy.

We are always at the mercy of speculation through highly educated guessing when attempting to predict or create the future; however, imagining the various possible outcomes based upon what has occurred in the past and what is occurring in the present is the most precise tool at our disposal. Robert C. Lieberman advises, "Rather, the idea of color blindness requires fleshing out in concrete contexts, and the working out of color-blind policies can actually paper over and perpetuate quite real racial distinctions and inequalities" (207-208). Proceeding with caution and directed zeal is critical for all concerned in assessing color blindness in theatre.

In the *African American Review's* Spring 2003 issue, Debby Thompson reviewed Anna Deavere Smith's performance of Carroll Smith-Rosenberg's *Is Race a Trope?* and claimed, "Many people, and particularly white, middle-class liberal humanists, want passionately to believe in and practice color-blind casting both onstage and in daily life. They want to believe that race is a 'mere' construct, and if we stop reconstructing it, it will go away. . . . Thus, liberal humanists often hear in Smith-Rosenberg's piece that race is not real—it's a trap—and are puzzled by what they see as the 'reverse racism' of Black Americans who insist on their own Black identity" (127). Race is not a "mere" construct in the debate on color blindness. In fact, it is at the center of the dispute. Although the voices of non-White proponents of non-traditional casting, like Rodney Douglas, cannot be dismissed, if attempts to understand the matter simply addresses artistic and policy measures (which do figure in the debate to a degree), the heart of the matter will be overlooked. Race is at the heart of the matter. And for reasons that were outlined in Chapter One, the main players are African Americans and White Americans, almost to the exclusion of other races. Every scholarly address on color blindness in theatre or in society at large has zeroed in on African Americans being ushered into White American theatre or society, mentioning Asian Americans, Native Americans, Latin Americans, and other marginalized groups incidentally. The nation's focus on these two primary groups indicates an urgent need for discourse between the two. So, we have to look to each group's acceptance or rejection of the notion. It is impossible to speak for every member of a cultural entity when addressing group views, however, the issue is overwhelmingly divided along African and White color lines.

What are the vested interests of the predominantly White American support for the use of color blindness as a social developmental tool? Robert Brustein provided some specific views in his 1996 TCG article. Although he is not the spokesperson for all of White American (as Wilson is not the spokesperson for all African Americans), Brustein has been the most outspoken. Much of the critical response from White American practitioners in Chapter One and this Chapter has mirrored his views. Brustein wants theatre to be a medium to which Whites can relate. "The foundation of this long tirade ["The Ground on Which I Stand"] is

Wilson's insistence on Black culture, particularly Black theatre, not only as an unparalleled achievement but also as a singular and discrete experience of life. It is an experience that cannot be fully absorbed or understood by white people, much less criticized by them. . . ." ("Subsidized Racism" 26). For this reason he sees Wilson's view of African American theatre as an attitude of exclusion toward Whites. During the Town Hall debate Brustein criticized *Bring in 'Da Noise, Bring in 'Da Funk* for not including the contributions of non-Black dancers (namely the Irish and Germans) in the history of tap dance. He is concerned about the loss of White American participation, contribution, and perhaps appreciation.

> I fear Wilson is displaying a failure of memory—I hesitate to say a failure of gratitude—when he charges nonprofit resident theatres with using "sociological criteria" in choosing seasons that "traditionally exclude Blacks." All of his own plays were originated and produced by a large consortium of mainstream institutions, including the Yale Repertory Theatre, the Huntington, the American Conservatory Theater, the Goodman, the Mark Taper, and so on. Wilson's pervasive tone of victimization, in fact, is oddly inappropriate for a playwright whose six LORT-generated plays, after completing the resident theatre circuit, all found their way to Broadway, where they won two Pulitzer Prizes, five New York Drama Critics Circle awards, and I don't know how many Tonys, besides generating enormous box-office income for the playwright (from white and Black audiences alike). Is a man who has garnered such extraordinary media attention (not to mention every conceivable playwriting fellowship) really in a position to say that Blacks are being excluded from the American theatre or that these institutions only 'preserve, promote and perpetuate white culture?' ("Subsidized Racism" 27)

Brustein also imagines an amalgamated world whereby African Americans are integrated into White society. "Are Black actors now to perform only Black parts written by Black playwrights? Will James Earl Jones no longer have a chance to play Judge Brack or Darth Vader? Must we bar Andre Braugher and Denzel Washington from enacting the Shakespearean monarchs? Is Othello not to be an acceptable opportunity for Morgan Freeman or Lawrence [sic] Fishburne? . . . No more *Voodoo Macbeths* or all-Black *Godot*s?" ("Subsidized Racism" 27)

A January 1997 editorial to The Boston Globe expresses similar desires to see African Americans more fully and freely sharing the drama of mainstream America:

> Both men are right, although we'd quarrel with Wilson on his view of non-traditional casting: Plays from Shakespeare to Arthur Miller are enriched by ethnic diversity. (Nunns" 19)

The writer quoted above had no qualms about African American theatre, as expressed in a following passage. It is significant however, that the writer equates non-traditional casting with the act of incorporating ethnic actors into White drama. Like Brustein's view, this perspective expresses a desire to see the integration of ethnic "others" into White society.

In refuting Wilson's charge that color blind casting is problematic because it ignores race, Patti Hartigan of The Boston Globe replied, "That is not entirely accurate, as Brustein points out. ART [American Repertory Theatre], in fact, has mounted countless productions of classics and contemporary dramas that were given new and profound resonance because of the casting of women or actors of color in roles traditionally played by white men" (E3). Again, the statement indicates a view of African Americans and other marginalized groups as being unquestioningly integrated into a larger society. This view spans across other professional fields, as well. Lieberman quotes social scientist Nathan Glazer, whom he calls, "one of the prophets of color blindness in the 1960s and 1970s." Glazer says:

One could believe that American Blacks would follow the path of European immigrants, now that state-imposed restrictions were lifted and private discrimination in key areas was banned . . . (203)

Indeed, integration of "cultural others" had always been the overriding goal of the early pioneers in color blind and non-traditional theatre. It was the goal of the Greenwich Mews Theatre with its series of integrated offerings in 1952 and it was certainly the goal of Joseph Papp for nearly half a century. The NTCP sought the same goals in the 1980s but saw conscious integration as merely a segue into unconscious inclusion whereby concerted efforts would evolve into a natural act of acceptance. "We called ourselves a 'project' because we hoped (and hope) to be short-lived, to act as a catalyst for change, rather than become an institution interested primarily in self perpetuation" (Newman 24). The NTCP envisioned a world that embraced full participation of cultural others with an acknowledgment and acceptance of diverse groups. The project sought to "forge a truly American performing arts" (Newman 22). "Since so much of our knowledge, understanding, and compassion for the world is shaped by theatre, film, and television, the absence of full and satisfying roles (in the largest meaning of that word) for these disenfranchised artists has had the insidious effect of reinforcing a view of a homogenous American society that has never been more than a fantasy" (Newman 23).

In the face of such noble goals and genuine concern for cultural others, it hardly seems congenial to not offer full societal cooperation. To discount the decades of resistance by African Americans and other cultural groups is socially remiss. In doing so, we designate advocates of non-traditional casting as the one voice for all. Furthermore, we have only addressed one, perhaps less crucial, aspect of the issue. As Williams asserts, "But if indeed it's not that easy then the application of such quick fixes becomes not just a shortcut but a short-circuiting of the process of resolution" (4). Brustein trivialized Wilson's position as mere victimization and petty revenge.

I am also disturbed by other attitudes reflected in that speech [TCG Address], notably that only the Black experience inspires the work of Black artists. . . . It is perfectly possible that I am wrong in my assessments. And I can understand how a playwright, no matter how highly praised by mainstream critics, can smart under adverse criticism, even in a relatively small-circulation periodical such as *The New Republic*. It is also no doubt painful to him that *Seven Guitars* lost the Tony this year to *Master Class*. But that is no justification for wheeling out the creaky juggernaut of Black Power to roll over any critic who makes a negative judgment on his plays. ("Subsidized Racism" 27)

Brustein attributes Wilson's politics to the sour grapes of a disgruntled playwright whose work was unfavorably criticized. His statements indicate a lack of concern for the apprehensiveness of Wilson and many other ethnic artists who feel that color blind casting has potential detrimental effects on culturally specific theatre. As Margo Hendricks states in "Gestures of Performance," "The idea of colorblind or nontraditional casting, not surprisingly, has its more vocal critics among the groups that are most often marginalized in United States theatre" (Thompson 190-191). These artists' concerns cannot be dismissed by Brustein as mere sour grapes. As a nation and as a global society we have an obligation to hear one another, and certainly to attempt to factor in all social needs and concerns, particularly when outcome and policy-making greatly impacts a significant segment of society.

How do African Americans who are against or who are not in complete favor of color blind and non-traditional casting practices in theatre envision their world in mainstream theatre? For some artists of color, color blind casting is a necessary economic evil. Wilson reported, "Some of my actors in (the Broadway cast of) 'Seven Guitars' said, 'If it weren't for colorblind casting, I wouldn't have worked'" (Hulbert 03B). In such cases, politics can take a back seat to finances. Wilson challenged those beliefs by stating, "I said, that's exactly my point. Why should you play a role that makes you mimic another group's speech and behavior in a (white-run theater) that does not take into account your history and the things that are of value in you as a person?" (Hulbert 03B). Essentially, Wilson was taking his actors to task for trading in heritage for a paycheck. From his statements we can also garner that he values and envisions a theatre experience that portrays the outer signs of ethnicity (speech and behavior), the honoring of and allegiance to heritage, and the incorporation of particular mores pertaining to his ethnic group. Ricardo Khan, artistic director of Crossroads Theatre Company, the only African American LORT company, envisions a pluralistic world, which he states is very different from a multi-cultural or color blind world, where we are "lifted all of us from a place of stagnation and cultural myopia to higher ground, where by design we set out to erase cultural presumptions and social stupidity" ("On Cultural Power" 15). Khan imagines a theatre world that "illuminates and celebrates cultural and ethnic distinction" rather than blurring the lines of race or creating a cultural interchangeability ("On Cultural Power" 15). Woodie King, Jr., producing director of the New Federal Theatre in New York visualizes an increased number of African American LORT theatres in a push for cultural particularism. "It would sound so much better to hear: Of the 76 LORT theatres, 11 are Black!" ("On Cultural Power" 59). In his vision for the Alliance Theatre Company, artistic director Kenny Leon focuses on "respect for the many voices of humanity, and cultural and generational inclusivity" ("On Cultural Power" 17). He has imagined and realized a world where marginalized groups are drawn into the theatre experience as artists, administrators, and audience through selecting material that speaks to these groups, through community outreach, marketing, and diversity in hiring practices.

At the heart of the matter, for both groups, is a desire to not be excluded. However, exclusion is viewed differently by proponents and critics of color blind casting. Each group has specific answers to the concern about exclusion. Supporters, mainly White Americans, are concerned that aspects of African American particularism in theatre will lead to a loss of White involvement as the ability to relate to this type of theatre is diminished. There is also indication of an unwillingness to support the funding of ventures that are outside of White America's experiential realm in the earlier-mentioned critical responses of Rogoff and

Brustein. Supporters of color blindness say, "Come join us. You have the right to be represented in American society and art. We can provide the vehicles. You just have to have talent and show up." This is evident in how the term color blind is defined. Journalist Vit Wagner stated, "At minimum, color-blind casting means allowing non-white actors to play characters not specifically written down as Black or Asian – an innocuous, inclusionary gesture that seemed radical even a decade ago, but is gradually finding more widespread acceptance" (k3). Wagner's statement reveals two significant points: a) color blind casting is seen as a practice that begins in a White arena which is entered by Black, Asian, and other previously excluded groups: and b) Whites are extending a privilege in "allowing" this entry. In fact, in most references to color blind casting by Whites the concept is equated with African Americans becoming part of the larger, White picture. All good intentions of shared representation aside, this perspective imagines a world that is dangerously lopsided. This is not to say that we should return to the days of minstrelsy and blackface, giving White performers equal cross-cultural time onstage. Rather, there is an inherent problem in a concept that is only acceptable from one cultural standpoint. Its function is no longer universal, at that point, and critical social problems are apt to arise if attempts are made at universal applications. Such is the predicament with color blind casting. Its limited social range has presented three pressing concerns in society.

The first concern is that color blindness has a potential toward obliteration of race distinction. Artists, educators, political scientists, sociologists, and leaders in a variety of other fields are apprehensive of what has been labeled "whitewashing race." In a 2003 book of the same name, seven scholars discuss the pitfalls of a color blind society. They state:

> In rejecting race-conscious classifications or remedies, the Court adheres to a jurisprudence of color-blindness that made sense in the 1950s and 1960s when segregation was legal and was based on a rigid system of racial classification.   Color-blindness undermined and transformed that system. But fifty years later when state-

sanctioned racial segregation is illegal and people of color have still to achieve truly equal opportunity with white Americans, the color-blind ideal actually impedes efforts necessary to eliminate racial inequality. Formal color-blindness fails to recognize or address the deeply rooted institutional practices and long-term disaccumulation that sustains racial inequality. Color-blind ideology is no longer a weapon that challenges racial inequality. Instead, it has become a powerful sword and a near-impenetrable shield, almost a civic religion, that actually promotes the unequal racial status quo. (Brown et al. 25)

How has color blindness, as a principle, promoted inequality according to the experts? There are assertions that color blindness serves as a social-political mask that (with or without hidden agendas) camouflages the reality of White privilege. The idea of White privilege is based upon inequality and imbalance of power. If it is camouflaged by a false sense of equal representation racism cannot be addressed. Color blindness is the blindfold that allows for the permeation and proliferation of racism. Ignoring race may provide the environment for ignoring racism.

What is being hidden in theatre by color blind casting? The glaring problem of White American drama superceding African American drama. Color blindness assumes the premise that the distance between cultures must be traversed by African Americans. White drama has become, in the minds of most practitioners, the vehicle by which African Americans enter a White domain to foster a more color blind world. Wilson says, "The idea of colorblind casting is the same idea of assimilation that African Americans have been rejecting for the past 380 years" ("Ground on Which I Stand" 72).

The fact of one group's artistic dominance over another leads to another key problem brought forth by color blind ideals. There is a false sense of social and artistic balance cultivated by color blind objectives. Many adherents claim that color blindness, as the wave of the future, brings cultures together in a spirit of reciprocal exchange. True, projects that utilize diverse groups of performers and personnel help create an environment for inter-cultural dialogue, and philosophical and experiential trade. Those incidental benefits, however important, do not create a balanced cultural society. Nor do the benefits help society to understand the need for upsetting the imperialistic status quo. Being physically in the same space, having a representative visual balance, is not the same as having a culturally balanced experience. Many color blind projects using classics and other White or European drama to showcase African American talent provide only a superficial representation of our diverse world. True diversity means creating a balanced amalgam of different cultures. It requires mentally and physically prioritizing the world around the balance. Once the belief system is in place, the actions will follow.

The third concern with color blindness posing social problems is of particular interest to political scientist Robert C. Lieberman. He assesses the situation thus:

> The dilemma affects other issues, as well, including education, housing and community development, and election reform, among others. In each of these issue areas, policy choices and outcomes will have consequences for the incorporation of minorities into national life. In each of these policy areas as well as others, strong claims are made about the virtues of color blindness both as a cultural and political ideal and as a policy strategy. But such blanket claims need careful empirical investigation to uncover the ways in which color blindness might or might not perpetuate racial inequalities through political mechanisms. . . . Color blindness, in other words, may have decidedly race-laden consequences. (223)

Lieberman, like many other White Americans, equates color blindness with the act of incorporating marginalized others into White society and is in favor of a color blind social structure. However, he also sees the potential for abuse in our society that, for a number of reasons, has an established history of political and economic imbalances of power between its cultural groups over the past 400 years. The potential for abuse can be seen in the problematic ethnocentrism of White American society more than in any specific intentions to further marginalize minority cultures. Ethnocentrism is harmful because it blinds one culture to the value of another culture in a patronizing, myopic march toward self-assertion. The very nature of this view is problematic for a genuine multi-cultural society that should experience more than visual variations of skin hues. The potential for abuse of power that Lieberman fears may grow naturally out of these ethnocentric views. If society is seen and experienced primarily through the lens of one group, then that group becomes the dominant influence. Coupled with political and economic dominance over all other groups, public policy-making has the strong potential to become skewed in favor of the prevailing group's interests. American theatre brings this dilemma to light. Until the mid 20th century American theatre sought to exclude African Americans and other minorities from mainstream theatre in favor of promoting White American/European theatre and its artists. With the advent of non-traditional casting, American theater has sought to include African Americans and other minorities in mainstream theatre but still largely in favor of promoting White American and European theatre. As Ania Loomba asserts, "Blindness to difference is often blindness to inequality, just as 'inclusion' can often be on terms that reinforce existing hierarchies, a point that has often been made in debates about secularism, multiculturalism, and antiracism in various contexts" (Thompson xvi).

Exclusion from America's artistic, social, and political arenas is a concern for many African American artists as well. It is an exclusion of culture rather than an exclusion of physical presence that troubles African American artists. As mentioned earlier, there is great concern about the representation and preservation of African American culture on the American stage. Opposition to color blind ideals is centered ultimately on exclusion of others'cultural identity from society. Detractors have communicated that, "We do not wish to show up on your doorstep. We do have the right to be fairly represented in American society and art; however, we wish to provide our own vehicles." These sentiments are evidenced in the following statement by actress Lisa Gay Hamilton in 1997:

> I have come to a place in my own career where I'm beginning to rethink what I really want. I have spent all of my life, literally, fighting to get into white institutions, fighting to get into white plays, arguing that I have every right to be there. And I've come to that place where I think that's pretty stupid. (Gold 2)

Sociologists such as Tommie Shelby have labeled this cultural identification as "Black cultural particularism." Shelby outlines the tradition as having eight basic tenets:

a) Blacks have a distinctive culture
b) Blacks should collectively and consciously reclaim that culture
c) Blacks should take pride in conserving and reproducing it [their culture].
d) Black culture provides a valuable foundation for their [Blacks'] individual and communal identities
e) Black culture is an emancipatory tool in resisting White hegemony, providing an alternate set of ideals to live by
f) Black culture should be accorded public recognition by the state
g) Blacks, as the main producers of this culture, should benefit from it in financial and other ways
h) Blacks, as owners of this culture, should be the foremost authorities and interpreters of it. (Patterson 2)

To many, Black cultural particularism sounds much like separatism. Black cultural particularism mirrors the assertions made by Wilson in his TCG address in 1996 which caused Brustein to label him a separatist in the 1997 responding article. Wilson adamantly denies being a separatist, which he made abundantly clear in the following passage:

> To pursue our cultural expression does not separate us. We are not separatists, as Mr. Brustein asserts. We are Americans trying to fulfill our talents. We are not the servants at the party. We are not apprentices in the kitchens. We are not stableboys to the King's huntsmen. We are Blacks. We are Americans. The irreversible sweep of history has decreed that. We are artists who seek to develop our talents and give expression to our personalities. We bring advantage to the common ground that is the American theatre. ("Ground on Which I Stand" 73)

Psychologist Daudi Ajani ya Azibo asserts:

> Irene Atwell and Daudi Ajani ya Azibo
> conceptualize that Black/Black Americans have
> normal or correct personalities when they have
> beliefs, values, attitudes and behaviors that are
> Black oriented; recognize themselves as Black and
> Black American; prioritize the interests, survival
> and proactive development of Black/Black
> Americans; and support a standard of conduct that
> neutralizes people and things that are anti-Black.
> The objective of this Black normalcy concept is
> not meant to be ethnocentric or anti-others, but to
> recognize the potential of psychological
> dysfunctioning which often results from an anti-
> self personality. Pro-self or pro-own group does
> not necessarily translate into being anti-others.
> (26-27)

Connected to the fear of losing cultural identity in the arts and other social arenas is the fear of losing identity through an erasure of racial identifiers. Loomba states, "Not surprisingly, it is precisely those who do not feel that race can be simply 'left at the door' who have challenged the idea that colorblind casting necessarily erodes racial difference, including, most famously, the playwright August Wilson" (Thompson xv-xvi). Nowhere is this concern more evident than in the American enslavement of Africans. There are social and behavioral theorists who argue that slavery erased African identity and that African Americans became a blank cultural slate inscribed with White American cultural values and customs. Kenneth Stampp, in his 1956 study on slavery says, "I have assumed that the slaves were merely ordinary human beings [and] that innately Negroes *are* only white men with black skins, nothing more, nothing less" (vii). Sociologist David De Camp wrote in 1949, ". . . that whatever language and culture the slaves had brought with them from Africa had been totally obliterated on the plantations and that the entire African race had had to start over again from scratch, this time under the tutelage of the white masters" Turner vi). Even more disturbing, some have believed that Africans brought to the States had no cultural identity. According to Richard L. Allen, "The racial conditions in the Americas, particularly in the United States, followed from earlier attitudes about Africans, such as the myths that Africans had no history and no written language" (25). This "blank slate" theory was introduced by Sidney Mintz in the early 1940s (Herskovits xviii). How pervasive is this outmoded thinking in today's society? That is difficult to gauge, but the prevailing attitudes of White American theatre artists about African American inclusion in White American/European drama suggest that there is still a lack of comprehension regarding the existence and necessity for a distinct African American culture. We have only to look to the artistic- and social-identification development of African Americans to understand why clinging to cultural particularism is of utmost importance to those who would reject color blind casting. In this chapter the exploration of the functionality of color blind practices for both White Americans and African Americans has revealed a vast chasm of differences in how the practice has been received and the investment of each group in the outcome. White Americans have generally seen color blind casting as a means of bringing marginalized groups into their world. African Americans have seen color blind casting as a potential means of excluding African American culture.

The task of weighing out the investments to decide where America should place its financial and artistic support in the matter is daunting, yet doable. There are only three major choices – a world with all color blind casting, a world with no color blind casting, and a world with a combination of color blind casting practices. It is safe to say, at this juncture, that all concerns, on both sides of the issue, are viable and should be factored into all decisions in a global attempt to fairly make use of the practice. In the concluding chapter prescriptions for its use that might serve as a meeting ground for the needs of both groups will be investigated. Our efforts will surely impact all future generations.

Before exploring equitable solutions, a balanced scale, in terms of how America views and accepts African American culture, should be established. Up to this point in American theatre, African American cultural pursuits have largely been relegated to a secondary status as evidenced in the disproportionate number of White/European dramatic productions that have brought African Americans into a color blind experience and the fact that African Americans comprise over twelve percent of the population yet can only claim less than a half percent of all LORT theatres. Toward this end, Chapter Three of this work explores the efforts of African Americans in retaining past cultural and theatrical identity and forging new identities from the time of arrival on American shores until the period just prior to the Black Arts Movement of the 1960s and 1970s. I found this to be a critical cut-off point. The very first responses to color blind practices from African American artists were offered at this juncture. It seems necessary to investigate how African American artistic and social development led to the first critical responses. The Black Arts Movement, revolutionary in nature and led by such powerhouses as Amiri Baraka, Ed Bullins, and activist Stokely Carmichael was more focused on intra-cultural development and less on establishing a new inter-cultural dialogic. While it would be fascinating and useful (in another context) to examine how color blind ideals were addressed throughout the Black Arts Movement period and its development into the 21st century, only a second volume could satisfactorily present its full scope.

Chapter Three

AFRICAN AMERICAN CULTURAL AND DRAMATIC
FORMATIONS IN AMERICA

*A renaissance of American Negro literature is due. The material about us
in the strange, heart-rending race tangle, is rich beyond dreams and only
we can tell the tale and sing the song from the heart.* W. E. B. DuBois

We can never fully comprehend how to position artistic practices and
ideals based upon the concept of a color blind society until we understand
in detail how life and culture were formed from the roots of African
Americans to the development of an African American culture in the
United States.

Richard L. Allen, in his work *The Concept of Self: A Study of Black
Identity and Self Esteem* posits, " . . . that the enslavement of Blacks had
major repercussions that are manifest even today and that it is impossible
to understand the social, political, and cultural history of Blacks in the
United States without understanding what happened before and after the
holocaust of slavery" (18). One's sense of identity is bound to the aspects
of life that define us, namely family, class, social practices, religious
beliefs and practices, gender, and other demographics. All that we identify
with in life serves to form our self-concepts, as will be mapped out in
Chapter Four. African American identity was initially imposed through
the assignations of White Americans at the time of captivity in Africa and
more fully at the time of arrival on American soil. This was an attempt to
reassign identity. As will be discovered, there was great resistance to being
re-identified and African Americans retained their drive toward self-
definition. To best discover the overall cultural intentions and needs of
African Americans in the past, present, and future, we must first return to
the origins of African American cultural identity to see the effects of
imposed White definitions and the establishment of self-definitions. This
chapter will focus on the developments in African American cultural and
theatrical identity from enslavement to the first official use of color blind
practices by the Greenwich Mews Theatre in 1953. At this point in history,
African Americans began speaking out against color blind casting (as
discussed in Chapter One), and the debate over its merits began.

African slave trading in America between the 17th and 20th centuries marks the greatest incidence of identity theft in the history of civilization. Mark Knowles states that in the four centuries of the Atlantic Slave Trade more than ten million Africans were unfortunate enough to be ensnared in the politics and economics of European and American slave traders (25). They were marched from their native lands and their identities toward their destinies of re-identification. According to videographers Ann E. Johnson and Robin Klein, by the time Africans reached the Western shores of Senegal, Mali, and the Ivory Coast from the interior lands, they had been stripped of their tribal garments, their grigri, or spiritual talismans, their tribal decorations, and their language ("Gorèe"). Upon arrival onto American shores, all outward vestiges of African culture and identity would be abruptly stripped away.

The first slaves were seized in raids upon small villages off the Western coast of Africa. Captors also picked up Africans who were caught alone and unaware. Early captives had the benefit of mutual support from fellow villagers who spoke the same languages. The long march from the villages-sometimes many days of travel- to the holding areas off the coast of Senegal, Guinea, and the Congo, afforded Africans a few opportunities to exchange communications. Plotting escapes was difficult but more possible in the earliest years of slave trading. As America grew and the need for labor increased exponentially, the need for greater shipments of Africans became necessary. The raiding of villages became less practical and far less safe as word spread throughout the tribes and African natives sought to protect themselves. Slave traders soon found ways to increase their cargo loads and avoid risking their own lives. The Portuguese, British, French, and Dutch had been conducting trade with wealthy African monarchs since the 15th century. But the first step of the later Atlantic Slave Trade after the 18th century was to convince African rulers to form mutually beneficial partnerships through the trading of fellow Africans. The second step was to encourage tribes to war against one another and to make prisoners of the defeated groups, thereby creating a large commodity pool. Tribal leaders would bring whole villages of captive Africans to the slave traders who would then transport the various groups to the holding Island of Gorèe. It became a much more efficient means of slave trading without the risks of venturing into the interior regions. However, the huge pool of human merchandise was made up of Africans from a variety of tribes. Language barriers interfered with the captives' ability to establish inter-tribal communication. Yoruba, Wolof, Lebo, and Bantu, among many other languages were spoken by the captives. Many captives were multi-lingual but for the vast majority, inter-communication was problematic.

> In Africa their cultures were rich and varied,
> as different from one another as were the African
> peoples themselves. Their colors, their languages,
> their food, their clothing differed in a range as great
> as the difference in size between the pygmies and the
> giant Watusi of Africa. (Meltzer 1)

The process of deleting identity involved a loss of physical heritage in the form of garments, ornamentation, language, and ritual. It was not complete until Africans reached the shores of America. The Middle Passage, described by historian Basil Davidson as "horrific," was the period of travel aboard the slave ships between Africa and the Americas. (*xv*) It was a waiting period where former identity began to fall away in the holds of the ships. It was also a time and place to understand how some Africans became fatally caught between the process of identity loss and the process of receiving new identities. Those individuals who could not transition from one process to the other threw themselves overboard at opportune moments. Traders and their ship crews lost a great deal of cargo in the early years of mass transport. Some loss was inevitable due to rough travel conditions that often took months. Disease was unavoidable as many Africans had little immunity to the germs of the foreigners. Certain preventive measures did help the traders to minimize their losses, however. They found that regular exercise and fresh air helped boost the health of the Africans who were brought aboveboard and compelled to sing and dance. Sailors brought out fiddles and were provided with comic entertainment as ailing Africans attempted to put tribal movement to European rhythms. Reluctant performers were whipped.

White America was introduced to the performing abilities of African slaves as early a 1664. The deck of the English slaveship Hannibal served as a stage for the imprisoned slaves, whose "daily exercise" was to be forced to sing and dance for the crew. The crew found them highly entertaining, as did the slave masters who later purchased them. But the habits, customs, and emotions that the slaves expressed in this entertainment showed that they were a people with a rich heritage; the demands would have a significant impact on their contribution to American culture. (Seller 37)

This was the pivotal moment when African identity began to meld with European/Anglo identity to form the uniquely African-American culture that exists today. Mark Knowles, in his book *Tap Roots: The Early History of Tap Dancing*, remarked, "Frequently slaves were forced to mimic the dances of the Irish and English crew, and this could have been one of the first cross-pollinations of European and African cultural styles" (26).

America - Re-identification

Self -identity takes place on both an inner and outer level. Outer identity revolves around our looks, names, languages, and physical behaviors, which, of course, are fueled by our inner identities based on beliefs, ideals, and so forth. By the time slave trading became an established business in the early 1700s removal of African identity began with an outer identity reformation when they reached the shores of Southern America and officially became slaves. Africans were cleaned, physically examined, and put on the auction block for sale. New, American names were distributed and taught through rote memorization. Physical punishment was administered to reluctant Africans. Likewise, physical punishment kept Africans from speaking their native languages or attempting to communicate with fellow Africans in their native languages. Africans were given American clothes to hide their "foul nakedness before God and man . . ." ("Gorèe").

To further remove ties with outer identity and to begin the process of inner-re-identity, familial ties were broken. By separating immediate family members and relatives in the selling process, any bonds that might encourage mutual emotional or psychological support were severed. Thus, resistance to new lives, new identities, or the reluctance to discard old identities could more easily be discouraged.

By the late 18th century the Atlantic slave trading business had peaked in America and strictly enforced rules against all African practices were firmly in place. Former Africans and their offspring were successfully re-identified as practicing and English speaking American property. Newly arrived Africans were quickly taught the re-identification process by their owners, but more effectively by slaves, and absorbed into the American plantation system.

Slave owners saw the value in allowing slaves to entertain themselves in ways that indicated they were happy. Simultaneously, slaves saw the value in keeping their owners happy and entertained. When slaves, particularly househands, went about their chores singing ditties or performing jigs, this was testimony to their owners that they were not unhappy with their lot in life. Many slaveholders, mistresses and masters alike, seized upon opportunities to have in-house entertainment for themselves and their guests.

> Dem days barbecues was de mos' source of amusement
> fer ev'ybody, all de white folks and de darkies de whole
> day long. All de fiddlers from ev'ywhars come to Sardis
> and fiddle fer de dances at de barbecues. Dey had a
> platform built not fer from de barbecue table to dance
> on. Any darky dat could cut de buck and de pigeon wing
> was called up to de latform to perform fer ev'ybody.
> Wesley Jones, (Rawick 73).

> Marse Wiliam whistle like a partridge; den Miss Nellie
> play her pianny. I dance and Marse send fer me a sugar
> an butter biscuit. Marse git his banjo and he pick it fer
> me to sing 'On, Bob white, is your wheat ripe? No, no, not
> quite.' Dat when I lived as a little gal on Marse William's
> home tract, called Musgrove Tract. – Cordelia Anderson
> Jackson, (Rawick 7).

In the isolated arena of the cotton fields darker, more lamenting songs were sung – songs of longing for freedom and sometimes escape. Frederick W. Bond described the atmosphere thus, "Without these canticles, the slaves were bewildered and friendless. Their theme was 'Trouble don't last always' (1).

During the earliest periods of slavery, in the late 17th and early 18th centuries, there were fewer restrictions upon African ritual performance. It wasn't long before slave owners became alarmed by the feverish states that Africans fell into during their tribal dances. White Americans felt that these displays of heathen practice not only riled up the Africans but led them into discontent and even insurrection. By the early to mid 18th century dancing and any enactment of dramatic movement was limited to American-influenced forms and any type of movement that reflected African customs was strictly prohibited. On Sundays and Holidays, usually the only times that generous owners allotted as non-working days, slaves were encouraged to hold dances that included bastardized versions of European and American waltzes. In New Orleans, however, slaves were permitted to hold public dances based on African customs. These weekly events were held in a place called Congo Square between the hours of 2pm and 9pm on Sundays under the watch of White authorities. The event became a tourist attraction, drawing White Americans from various parts of the state, the country, and Europe. According to Knowles "White Americans, used to erect European dancing with recognizable footwork, were shocked and fascinated by these dances" (27). This was an unusual allowance that was not granted in any other slave-holding state or any other area of Louisiana, to the best of historical knowledge. But again, African American entertainment was limited to being performed for the pleasure of White Americans.

Slave owners also censored the religious practices of slaves, not recognizing African rituals as anything more than heathenism. It was widely believed that Africans had been saved from the heathenism of their dark continent in coming to America. Many missionaries were sent to Africa as early as the 16th century for just that purpose. This belief enabled Europeans and Americans to justify the mass relocation of Africans and the stripping away of their customs and rituals. Thus, Christianity was the only religion that could be practiced by slaves. Slaves learned the prayers, hymns, and ceremony of Christianity. Holding Americanized church services in English was the only means of congregating for African Americans. The harsh realities of slave life made the necessity of coming together for renewed faith and support a vital matter.

Consequently, African American expression in dance, song, language, and religious practice became a mandatory imitation of White American expression, a key process in re-identification. There is a distinct relationship between imitation and identity. Imitation often leads to identity creation as simulation behaviors become habitual practice, which result in identification and eventual self-description. This is not to say that African expression was completely lost – but it did become surreptitiously hidden and/or blended to create a unique integration of African and

American expression that is much of what we witness in African American art today – African American themes expressed through White American paradigms. But it would be a century from the height of the American slave trade in the late 1700s before African Americans could begin to express themselves artistically for their own social and psychological enrichment.

African Americans in the south were not able to perform for profit until post-slavery. With the exception of The African Company, and perhaps other isolated theatre ventures, Northern African Americans were largely invisible in theatre as well.

> From the Colonial period to the 1850s, there
> were no Negroes on the New York stage or in
> the audience . . . Black actors entered the commercial
> theatre through a side door labeled The Minstrel Show.
> (Archer 10)

African Americans jumped on the minstrelsy bandwagon, imitating Whites who were imitating African Americans, creating a circular parody in the process. Minstrelsy was, of course, a complete lampooning of African American characteristics. Post-emancipation African Americans had few employment opportunities outside of hard field labor that mostly mirrored the conditions and economic disadvantages of slavery. Entertaining Whites was a job they had always excelled at during slavery and proved to be profitable after slavery. After all, Southern Whites had laughed uproariously at the expense of African Americans since they first arrived in America as they attempted to obediently learn the strange new sounds, words, customs, and mannerisms of their owners. Often the laughter was centered on a slave's awkward physical movement while shackled or after crippling physical punishment. Slaves learned to accentuate the behaviorisms that brought on their owners' derisive amusement. The transition to minstrelsy was therefore easily facilitated. African Americans' willingness to place themselves in such derogatory roles was fueled by a need to survive economically and so a handful of notable African American minstrel troupes like the Georgia Minstrel Troupe and Lew Johnson's Plantation Minstrel Company were founded in the second half of the 19th century.

African Americans who were born free, freed or escaped, and living in the North were not under the same social and survival obligations as their formerly enslaved relations in the South. Northern African Americans began to create their own theatres and dramas about the turn of the 19th century. Most noteworthy and the earliest company on record was the African Company, headed by James Hewlett from 1820 until 1821. His company performed the first recorded non-traditional production of Shakespeare's *King Richard III*. It was non-traditional in the sense that it performed by an all-African American cast. The African Company's productions were initially performed for the African American population in New York, however, Whites began to show up in the theatre mainly to harass the performers. Whites also had objections to the segregated performances so the company held separate performances since Whites did not know "how to behave themselves at entertainment designed for ladies and gentlemen of colour" as the sign posted in the theatre read (Mitchell 25).

The African Company also presented some of the first plays written by and about African Americans. According to historian Marvin McAllister, the African Company "dared to challenge Manhattan's Park Theatre." The Park was Manhattan's previously undisputed "major" theater and was managed by Stephen Price, a lawyer who became America's first noteworthy theatrical producer. Price would prove an important and debilitating rival for Brown's upstart African American theater." Violence and police harassment caused the company to close in 1821 but the door had been opened to the creation of African American drama and performance and new plays and companies sprang up primarily in New York City.

This study is in agreement with David Krasner who stated in *Resistance, Parody, and Double Consciousness in African American Theatre, 1895-1910*, "In studying Black theatre, there is more at stake than mere chronological narrative; there are the ways in which Black theatre sought to change the perception of Blacks on the American stage" (3-4). In examining African American drama, companies, and performers from roughly the mid-1800s till the mid-1900s, an evolutionary trend reveals itself. The trend indicates the directions that were taken and what the directions indicate about the cultural needs of African Americans in art from that period till the formal introduction of color blind casting in the early 1950s.

Genevieve Fabre sees the intent of African American theatre throughout history as a polarized fluctuation between the need for integration and the need for autonomous freedom and self-expression (31). The efforts of The African Company seem to support Fabre's assertion, explaining in part why Shakespeare's works dominated their repertoire. Elizabeth Brown-Guillory attributes this phenomenon to a lack of written Black drama, explaining that African Americans come from an oral tradition out of Africa that took considerable time to evolve into a written tradition. Indeed, a strong oral tradition is the cornerstone of African culture. Mark Mathabane writes about the prevailing oral tradition in Africa in his autobiography, *Kaffir Boy*. The following excerpt reveals the full scope of how this oral tradition is at the center of African life and consequently, early African American life:

> My mother said that her stories had been handed down to her from past generations; and that, therefore, she was narrating them not only to entertain us children and to teach us morals, but also that we, in turn, would come to tell our children, and they, their children and so on through posterity. She was such a mesmerizing storyteller that once she began telling a tale, we children would remain so quiet under her hypnotic voice, that we would often hear ourselves breathing. Whenever she ended a particular story, saying that it was past our bedtime, we would implore her to tell another one – a request she always heartily granted – until either my father screamed from the bedroom that the candle be snuffed, or we children simply dozed off into faraway worlds, our minds pregnant with fantastic yarns we wished never to forget.
>
> My mother's vast knowledge of folklore, her vivid remembrance of traditions of various tribes of long ago and her uncanny ability to turn mere words into unforgettable pictures, fused night after night to concoct riveting stories.

On some nights, she would tell of chiefs, witch doctors, sages, warriors, sorcerers, magicians and wild, monstrous beasts. These stories were set in mythical African kingdoms ruled by African people where no white man had ever set foot. She would recount prodigious deeds of famous African gods, endowed with unlimited magical powers; among them the powers of immortality, invincibility and invisibility, powers which they used to fight, relentlessly and valiantly, for justice, peace and harmony among all African tribes of the Valley of a Thousand Hills.

On some nights, she would quaintly and proudly tell legends about great and noble chiefs of her tribe, the Tsongas; chiefs, who along with powerful chivalrous warrior, undertook many daring and perilous missions into the unknown interiors of Africa, and there fought many a brilliant battle against ferocious enemy tribes. When the battles were won, however, instead of subjugating the conquered people as other tribes did, the Tsonga impis always allowed the vanquished to continue following their old beliefs, customs and tradition, and to worship their own gods, as long as they pledged to live in peace with, and to pay homage to, their conquerors.

On some nights, she would tell stories abut animals. These animals, to whom she gave the complete gamut of human traits – strength, cowardice, love, hate, honesty, wisdom, magnanimity, cunning, treachery, fear and so on – behaved very much like humans, and she would highlight their interactions with human beings. The animals in her stories were always smarter than humans, and capable of making complex moral decisions.

And on some nights she would teach us tribal songs, proverbs and riddles, all of which she encouraged us to commit to memory, saying, "Memory to us African people is like a book that one can read over and over again for an entire lifetime."

As we had no nursery rhymes nor storybooks, and, besides, as no one in the house knew how to read, my mothers stories served as a kind of library, a golden fountain of knowledge where we children learned about right and wrong, about good and evil. (78-79)

The literacy issues for Africans mirrored the literacy issues for African Americans. But in America it became a central problem to the evolution of African American formal playwriting where the ability to read and write was a necessity not required in pre-colonial Africa.

Slaves were not permitted to learn, of course. The state of Mississippi enacted laws which prohibited the teaching of reading and writing to African Americans, as well as laws which prevented five or more free or enslaved African Americans from gathering together. The latter mandate interfered with the centuries old African public storytelling customs. Long after emancipation, many Southern African Americans remained illiterate. Consequently, much of African American writing of any form came out of the free states in the Midwest and the North. The life of escaped Kentuckian slave William Wells Brown, who authored *Escape or Leap for Freedom* was an exception to the rule. Brown learned to read and write from his liberal, educated master's son. He later was sent to Missouri where he ultimately worked as an apprentice for the editor of the *St. Louis Times*, Elijah Lovejoy. Although born a slave from a Southern state he was given a unique opportunity to gain literacy. Most African American dramatists of the 19th century, like Pauline Elizabeth Hopkins, Katherine D. Chapman Tillman, Mary Burrill, and Willis Richardson were born in Northern states or post-slavery.

Early African American Drama

Mance Williams categorizes the pre-emancipation period of African American drama as one of protest, and protest " . . . is what characterized the bulk of Black drama prior to the 1960s" (24). Fabre believes this period was a precursor to the militant Black Power drama of the 1950s and 1960s, " . . . when playwrights presented images of resistance and liberation" (31). African American drama before the turn of the century was not abundant but it defined the formation of an African American consciousness and as such requires a detailed inspection.

African American drama has always been political; a reaction to the social events of the period. Its themes have been directed toward intercultural protest, intra-cultural protest, or both. The earliest extant African American drama speaks directly to intercultural protest in its satirical message aimed at colonials. Mr. Brown's play, *The Drama of King Shotaway*, written in 1820 and based on the 1776 uprising of Black and Yellow Caribs against the English navy, dramatized the slave uprising on the Caribbean island of St. Vincent. There are no existing copies of the script, however, the element of protest against slave captivity is inherent in historical facts upon which the drama is based. According to the St. Vincent and Grenadines Department of Tourism, the play's author was, himself, a Black Carib purportedly involved in the insurrection of 1796. The Yellow Caribs who arrived on the island of St. Vincent in the early 16th century from South America effectively managed to keep the island from European invasion and colonization. The Black Caribs were Africans who landed on the island accidentally after surviving the sinking of a Dutch slave ship in 1635. After a number of battles both groups agreed to share the island, with the yellow Caribs taking the leeward side and the Black Caribs taking the windward side. In 1795 they banded together against British invasion with Chatoyer leading the Yellow Caribs and DuValle leading the Black Caribs in what was known as the Second Carib War. The Caribs on both sides were defeated and ultimately exiled to the island of Balliceaux. Chatoyer was killed in battle and became a national hero. The St. Vincent and Grenadines Department of Tourism believes *The Drama of King Shotaway* is a tribute to Chatoyer. Maxine Schwartz Seller refers to the drama as a ". . . sharp satire on the institution of slavery" (38-39). In writing about battles against colonialism in a foreign context, Brown avoids a direct indictment against American politics yet the correlation to the social and political plight of African Americans is unavoidably evident.

Intercultural protest is also a thematic focus of William Wells Brown's 1858 *The Escape or Leap for Freedom*, which is an account of his own life as a slave. But a strong element of intra-cultural protest underscores the story. Brown was a dedicated abolitionist who also wrote the first African American novel. He later became a lecturer and historian. He was born into slavery on the plantation of John Young, a physician in Kentucky. *Escape* is a social satire about the American institution of slavery. The plot is based on the concept of human beings as property, as passed down by the United States Supreme Court. In 1857 the federal government declared that escaped slaves remained the property of their owners, to be returned forthwith. The drama was never staged as a production but was published and presented as a reading by Brown in Salem, Ohio on February 4, 1847 and was well-received. Leo Hamalian and James V. Hatch have commented on Brown's courage in presenting a subject that was taboo and illegal at that point in history (39). The script was lost and rediscovered in 1968 by Doris Abramson (Seller 39). This stroke of fortune has provided scholars with a unique opportunity to examine the social protest of early African American dramatic writing.

The character of Cato, who Hamalian and Hatch refer to as a reformed Uncle Tom, reclaims his identity as he joins other escaping slaves in the final scene. James V. Hatch asserts, "By this leap for freedom, Cato becomes a human being" (Hatch and Shine 34).

> Cato: Ah, chile, I come wid ole massa to hunt you;
> an' you see I get tired huntin' you , an' I am now
> huntin' for Canada. I leff de ole boss in de bed at
> de hotel; an' you see I thought, afore I left massa,
> I'd jess change clothes wid him; so, you see, I
> is fexed up – ha, ha, ha. Ah, chillen! I is gwine wid you.
> (Hatch and Shine 54)

Cato's declaration reaffirms the idea that even the demoralized slave can find sufficient fortitude to set himself mentally and physically free.

Brown strengthens his politics by presenting a slave who converts from former cooperation with the institution of slavery to self-preservation. He garners further support for his ideals by closing the drama with verbal and physical protest from a White supporter.

> Mr. White: Why, Bless me! These are the
> slaveholding fellows. I'll fight for freedom!
> (*takes hold of his umbrella with both hands.*
> *The fight commences in which* Glen, Cato,
> Dr Gaines, Scragg, White, *and* the officers
> *take part.* Dr. Gaines, Scragg, *and* the officers
> *are knocked down.* (Hatch and Shine 58)

Mr. White is not only cunningly named but also artfully positioned as an upstanding citizen from Massachusetts, in sharp contrast to plantation owner Dr. Gaines, his wife, clergyman John Pinchen, and the overseer who are all despicable bigots. The distinction illustrates the author's experiences with the slave-holding Whites of the South and the abolitionist sympathizers of the North. Brown also makes the act of protest one of decisive triumph, not the plea for understanding and tolerance that Brown-Guillory states was the mark of the early protest plays, ". . . that made an appeal for justice for African Americans "(2). Glen and Melinda battle the slave hunters before jumping into the escaping boat. They literally "leap for freedom." Mr. and Mrs. Neal, the Quakers who aided their escape ask Thomas to sing a song he has written as they pull from shore.

> Mr. Neal: Well, Thomas, if thee has a ditty, thee
> may recite it to us.
>
> Thomas: Well, I'll give it to you. Remember that I
> call it, *The Underground Railroad.* (Hatch and Shine 56)

In the final lines, Brown offers Black and White Americans, alike, a triumphant protest.

> Glen, Melinda*, and* Cato *jump into the boat, and*
> *as it leaves the shore and floats away,* Glen *and* Cato
> *wave their hats, and shout loudly for freedom.*
> (Hatch and Shine 58)

Fabre asserts that African Americans have been and are pulled between two opposing forces – the need for integration and the need for autonomy. She further posits that in African American theatrical expression, "This legitimate desire for integration runs counter to the objective of freedom" (31). The intercultural protest against social and economic dependence in a bid for freedom characterized post-emancipation African American drama but is joined more intensively by an internal protest against African

American negativity by the end of the century. In Pauline Elizabeth Hopkins' 1879 drama *Peculiar Sam, or the Underground Railroad*, intra-cultural reform is decidedly specific. This drama deserves an in-depth analysis because it foreshadows a critical time in African American social and economic development and also a critical change in self-perception. The post-slavery era found emancipated slaves struggling to survive against tremendous odds and confused allegiances. However, by the last quarter of the century African Americans began to thrive on all levels. The period became a prosperous time in African American lives (a condition that would not be seen again until the mid 20th century) until the rise of White backlash in the form of the Ku Klux Klan at the close of the century. A recognition of the need for group collaboration in African America arose that was reflected in the drama of the time. By the turn of the century a new African American consciousness had arisen. David Krasner describes the period in the following passage:

> Black theatre from 1895 to 1910 in particular existed during a period of racial turmoil. Against this backdrop, Black Americans created and performed before both Black and whites. White racism and the Black solidarity that opposed it both played a significant role in establishing a collective consciousness among Black Americans that ultimately led to the realization of a Black social identity. This, in turn, yielded a Black aesthetic . . . (3)

Hopkins, like William Wells Brown, framed *Peculiar Sam, or the Underground Railroad* around a slave escape. Although the Emancipation Proclamation of 1863 freed all slaves in America, the author returned to the theme of slavery to illustrate the fact that African Americans at that time were bidding for the next level of freedom – social and economic autonomy. So much analysis is given to this drama because it marks: a) a call to action on the part of African Americans; b) a distinction between several types of African Americans who are progressive, regressive, or a combination of both in the African American's bid for autonomy;   c) the means by which African Americans can make bids for independence;   and d) the need for intra-cultural communication and cooperation.

Sam's peculiarity lies in the fact that he is unlike the other African American characters in the drama. He becomes a man of action against a backdrop of despair and frozen immobility. The other characters initially speak of his attribute with amusement and then admiration as his passion turns to action.

> Sam: Yas, we's all gwine to Canidy! Dars
> been suthin' a growin' an' a growin' inter
> me, an' it keep sayin', "Run 'way, run away,
> Sam. Be a man, be a free man."
> An' Mammy, ef it hadn't been fer you an'
> de gals I'd been gone long 'go. But Ise prepared
> myself, in kase ob a 'mergensy.
>
> Juno: I know whar dat is, dar aint no slabe niggers
> dar, dey's all token care on by Mrs. Queen Victoria,
> she's de Presidunt ob Canidy.
>
> Mammy: You hish up gal, an' laf your brudder talk.
> Day allers tol' me dat boy was pecooliar, but I neber
> 'spected it would revelop itself in dis way.
> (Hamalian, Hatch 105)

By the end of Act I, Sam has overpowered Jim, the African American overseer, who is his reason for planning an escape to Canada, and who is his main obstacle in realizing the plan. He has also assembled his mother, sister, and true love, Virginia, in preparation for the escape. When he reenters the scene he is holding the overseer's whip and his credibility goes up several notches in the eyes of his family.

> Mammy: Why, honey, I hardly know'd my own chile.
>
> Juno: What a peccoliar fellar you is! Look jes like a
> gemman. (Hamalian and Hatch 108)

72

In fact, a gentleman is what he becomes by the final act and his family realizes that his peculiarity lies, to a great extent, in his strong leadership capabilities, which make him decidedly different from the other African American males in the story. In Act IV, the entire party of escapees are settled comfortably in Canada owing to Sam's unflinching guidance and conviction that they all deserved freedom and abundance. The idea of his peculiarity is now spoken of in awe.

> Caesar: Ol' 'ooman it are a long time sense we an'
> de chillern lef' de ol' home, seems to me de Lor'
> has blessed us all. Hyars you an' me married, Jinny
> a singist, Juno a school marm; an' las' but not leas',
> dat boy, dat pecoolar Sam, eddicated an' gwine to de
> United States Congress. I tell you ol' 'ooman de ways
> ob de Lor' am pas' findin' out.

> Mammy: Yas ol' man, an' hyar we is dis blessed
> Christmas evenin', a settin' hyar like kings an' queens,
> waitin', fer dat blessed boy o' ours to come home to us.
> Tell you ol' man, it's 'mazin' how dat boy has 'scaped
> de gins an' sneers ob de worl', an' to-day am runnin' fer
> Congress dar in Cincinattie, it am 'mazin. D'ye s'pose
> he'll git it ol' man?

> Caesar: I don't spec' nothin' else, kase dat boy allers gits
> what he goes fer. (Hamalian and Hatch 119)

The title character is also so named because he has adopted a "by any means necessary" approach to attaining his goals. Sam's industriousness and determination lead him to rallying the only manpower he has – his family:

> Sam: Dars a mulatto fellar gwine to start a gang up
> river ton-night, an' Ise gwine to be dat fellar, an' you's
> gwine to be de gang. Ef we kin 'complish dis we's allright,

an' we'll say good-bye to the ole plantation. (Hamalian and Hatch 105)

The real test of his inventiveness lies in his getting around the central obstacle of Jim who is both his romantic rival for the hand of Virginia, and his barrier to freedom. Jim stands to be awarded one hundred dollars for the capture of Sam's "gang" of runaways. Jim is also driven by the fact that Sam will be taking Virginia on his escape and that he will be punished severely by the master if he doesn't detain the runaways. But Jim is no match for Sam's cunning aggression. Sam first bests Jim physically, taking the whip that Jim was intending to use on him. When Sam and his party meet their Underground Railroad contact, Caesar, he disguises himself as the old man so that Caesar can transport the ladies to a safer place.

> Sam: All right uncle, an' ef eny body cames, I reckon I can gib dem all de degamation dey wants. Now you jez han' ober dat dressum gown an' dat cap an' I'll reguise mysel' inter them. (*places wig and moustache in his pocket, exchanges his coat and hat for Caesars*). (Hamalian and Hatch 110)

The disguise allows him to fool Jim who arrives at the hut seeking information about the runaway slaves but it is Sam's comical bargaining with Jim that attests to his inventiveness. By the time they finish bartering, he has earned three dollars and Jim has been sent on a wild goose chase. But Jim has suspicions of his own about the false information received and returns in a ghost disguise to try to frighten the information out of Sam, who is still believed to be Caesar. Sam realizes the hoax and reverts back to physical aggression by overpowering and robbing Jim of the one hundred dollar reward money and a pistol before taking him hostage.

Hopkins portrays Sam's theft as a very practical necessity which loses its vice in light of the nefarious characters he is up against. The idea that one may have to "play unfair" for a higher cause is clearly being communicated by the author and she allows Sam his defense.

Mammy: (*more surprised*) Been stealin' too. (*groans*)
I neber 'spected dat ob you Sam.

Sam: No use Mammy, we mus' hab money, de
Litioners am good frien's to us, but money's ebery man's
frien', an'll neber 'tray eben a forsook coon. (Hamalian
and Hatch 118)

The need for intra-cultural reform is perhaps the drama's strongest bid. Hopkins juxtaposes four distinct "negro" types within one segment of society and allows the story to demonstrate how the four types work together effectively at furthering the goals of a disadvantaged race.

The tragic mulatto is a familiar character in early American drama. Dion Boucicault brought this character center stage in his 1859 tragedy, *The Octoroon*. Zoe, the Octoroon, has one-eighth of African blood which keeps her from exercising the rights and advantages of the White world although she is much beloved by that society. The real tragedy is that she is considered too Black to be White and too White to be Black, and is essentially an impotent character. Curtis describes the dilemma by stating, "Because the tragic mulatto operated mostly in a white world . . . the character did not explore Negro life as such" (56). Therefore, the character, usually a female, cannot assist in the furthering of African American ideals. The drama *Peculiar Sam*, however, utilizes a barely visible mulatto female with great power. Virginia is the force that propels the action through her influence on Sam. As the archetypal tragic mulatto she is not obsessed with her drop of Negro blood but she is carefully distinguished from the other characters by her racial status.

Mammy: . . . Yes, deys bring dat gal up like a lady, she
neber done nuthin' but jes wait on Marse fambly . . .

Sam: (*sorrowfully*) Po' little gal *(sings):*
Ah! Jinny is a simple chile,
Wif pretty shinin' curls,
An' white folks love her best, of all
The young mulatto girls. (Hamalian and Hatch 102-103)

Ironically, Sam and his sister, Juno, are mulattos, as well. Mulatto simply means that an African American is not of pure African blood. This accounted for a large portion of the African American population in the South at that time. But Virginia clearly has much more White blood and is given White characteristics that set her apart from the others. Her dialogue is written in standard American English without the African American vernacular that is spoken by the other characters.

> Virginia: While we are waiting for Sam let's
> sing again before we leave our old home. For
> though we leave it in darkness and sorrow, it is
> still our home. (Hamalian and Hatch 108)

Virginia serves to drive Sam toward his goals and in the end, she becomes his prize. Initially, Mammy brings the news of Virginia's forced marriage to Sam. Juno then brings the news that Virginia is planning to run away.

> Juno: Mammy, I jes toted Jinny down hyar, for
> you to use some salvation wif her; talk 'bout dat
> gal's bein' sof' and easy. She says she's gwine to
> run 'way to-night.

> Virginia: Yes, Mammy, and Sam, I have come to
> say good-bye, it's hard to leave the place where I was
> born, but it is better to do this, than to remain here, and
> become what they wish me to be. To fulfill this so-called
> marriage. (Hamalian and Hatch 104)

The announcement causes Sam to spring into action.

> Sam: Jinny, you isn't 'fraid to trust ol' peculiar Sam,
> I know, kase you see Ise allers willin' to die fer you.
> You needn't bid any on us good-bye, kase dis night
> I 'tends to tote you and Mammy and Juno way from

hyar. Yas, an' I'll neber drop ye till Ise toted you safe inter Canidy. (Hamalian and Hatch 104)

After the group has settled safely in Canada, there is still some concern about the fact that Jim is still on the loose, in search of the escaped party. Virginia cannot rest until Jim's whereabouts are known.

Juno: And just to think, if Sam's elected you'll be poppy to a representative, and Mammy'll be mother to one, and I'll be sister to one. (*to Virginia*) And what'll you be to him, Jinny?

Virginia: Don't talk about that Juno; there can be nothing done until Jim is found.

Sam: Haven't you one word for me, Virginia?

Virginia: Find Jim, and we will be happy. (Hamalian and Hatch 121)

Mammy and Juno are two characters who can be placed in the "slave mentality" category. They are carried to freedom through proactive measures taken by Sam but possess none of his vision about the rights of African Americans. Mammy believes in the glories of life in the hereafter where heaven rights all wrongs.

Mammy: . . . Don't yer gib up nor lose your spirits, for de Lord am comin' on his mighty chariot, drawn by his big white horse, an' de white folks hyar, am a gwine to tremble. Son Ise been waitin' dese twenty-five year, an' I aint guv up yet. (Hamalian and Hatch 103)

Mammy is not willing to take a stand against conditions in this world but she bears a distinct dignity and pride in her life on earth. Following Sam's declaration that he is going to run away, to be a free man, Mammy states, "Look hyar boy, . . .I doesn't want you to bring no disrace onter me (Act I). And Juno's self-racism prompts Mammy to admonish:

> Mammy: You Juno, hish, fer we's all His chillren, an He lubs us all. (Hamalian and Hatch 115)

Juno is much more steeped in despair and self-disgust:

> Juno: (*sorrowfully*) Dar aint no use tryin' to be like white folds, we's jus made fer nuthin' but igerant slabes, an' I jes b'lieve God don't want nuthin' to do wid us no how. . . . Mammy dey say angels am all white. How's I gwine to be a angel Mammy? I jes dn' 'lieve God wants eny brack angels, 'deed I dn', less 'tis to tote things for Him. (Hamalian and Hatch 114)

Not until they are all living the White dream, with a home, nice clothes, and Sam on his way to becoming a politician, does Juno leave behind the slave mentality and adopt a sense of self-confidence. Likewise, Mammy begins to believe in a life of hope on earth rather than heaven after all are safely established in Canada. They each, in small ways aid the escape, however. Mammy helps pave the way with Caesar, the Underground Railroad contact, and Juno uses her gun skills to provide the "muscle" that keeps Jim under guard.

Jim represents the "Uncle Tom" outlook that is seen as counterproductive to the goals of African Americans in search of freedom from inequality. As Loften Mitchell states, "An "Uncle Tom, "Tom" or "Uncle" is the most inflammatory, insulting thing a Black man can be called" (34). The term is derived directly from the title character of Harriet Beecher Stowe's 1852 novel that was adapted for the stage by George L.

Aiken in that same year. The character came to be known as both a paternalistically romantic creation by Whites and as a traitor to African American dignity. In the eyes of African Americans, Uncle Toms serve Whites without question or rancor even in light of extreme oppression. As the overseer who abuses the plantation's slaves and assists the owner in capturing escaped slaves, Jim is the "Tom" character. Sam draws the distinction between slaves like Jim and himself in the following passage:

> Jim: Ef you strike me, Marse'll skun you.
>
> Sam: (*contemptuously*) Marser's pet! Come on,
> you, you lizard hearted coon, we'll hab a set-to,
> for Ise boun' to take your sass out on your hide.
>
> Jim: O, ef I only had you tied to the widder!
>
> Sam: This thing is played out; as for havin' a common
> nigger talkin' 'bout tyin' me up, I isn't gwine to.
> I wouldn't be such a 'teriated coon as you is
> for all de Norf. (Hamalian and Hatch 106)

In the final act, after Lincoln's soldiers invaded the territory, a converted Jim has escaped and joined the group in Canada. He traveled to Massachusetts to get an education and became an attorney. In the glow of freedom all is forgiven.

Sam possesses the "Anti-slave" mentality; a man, who given half a chance, can parlay every opportunity into a gainful situation. All of the characters with the exception of Pete, Pomp, and Virginia undergo radical changes in outlook and position, however, Sam's progression is the greatest and is marked by a change in speech.

> Sam: Well Jim, I forgive you freely for all that's
> past and here's my hand on it. And now Virginia
> I await your answer, when shall our wedding take
> place? (Hamalian and Hatch 123)

Hopkins revises his language to reflect his new status as a future statesman but also to indicate how his strivings have reaped the reward of outward equality in the White world. But Sam maintains a sense of pride in his race that can never be forgotten in his climb toward the White American dream of manifest destiny. The final lines of the play indicate that Hopkins does not want African Americans to forget their roots.

> Juno: But Lor', I forgot, we can't dance anything
> but high-toned dances, we must remember that ther's the
> dignity of an M.C. to be upheld. But anyhow, you fellow
> have out the chairs and things, an' we'll have a quadrille.
>
> Sam: Ladies and gentlemen, I hope you will excuse me
> for laying aside the dignity of an elected M.C. and allow
> me to appear before you once more as peculiar Sam of the
> old underground railroad. (Hamalian and Hatch 123)

Hopkins directs the primary themes in her drama toward African Americans. The messages clearly communicate the need for all to work cohesively toward group freedom. By intertwining the lives of various character types, some at odds with one another and with the goals, the playwright makes the observation that African Americans are a heterogeneous group whose individuals come from many different life orientations. In the final analysis, Hopkins shows us that a collective conscious can be gained amongst opposing individuals so that all may reap the benefits. Her drama marks a trend toward using intra-cultural protest in drama to unite African Americans in late 19th century America while serving to remonstrate against inequality.

Turn of the Century Protest
Minstrelsy and vaudeville were as popular as ever in the late 19th century And provided much needed work for African American performers. However, by the mid- 1890s an anti-minstrelsy contingent of African American writers and performers sought to establish serious drama about

African Americans. John Isham wrote *The Octoroons* in 1895 which was the first African American musical that broke away from minstrelsy and burlesque. Bob Cole and J. Rosamond Johnson followed with what Loften Mitchell called "the first true Negro operetta," *Shoofly Regiment* in 1898, also a non-minstrel production, and William Cook wrote *Clorindy: The Origin of the Cakewalk* that same year with renowned African American poet Paul Lawrence Dunbar (47). Gerald Thomas Goodman described the latter two productions as "coon shows that departed from the minstrel formula and became musicals by adding plots and characters" (33). African American artists were attempting to define and present their culture for themselves rather than through the lens of White stereotyping.

The post-Emancipation Proclamation period was a time of social upheaval and confusion as America began the process of Reconstruction. The relationship between four million ex-slaves and their former owners was forced into re-definition. Leon F. Litwack attests, "When they [freed slaves] chose to test their freedom by entering public places from which they had previously been barred or by sitting indiscriminately in public conveyances where their presence had previously been restricted, the worst fears of the white South were realized and the utmost vigilance demanded" (261). African American Reconstruction also began in earnest. African American-owned restaurants, nightclubs, hotels, and other businesses sprang up in Northern and Southern towns and cities. African American invention was on the rise. Entrepreneurs like Madame C. J. Walker who was one of America's earliest self-made women millionaires, began acquiring real estate, national businesses, and noticeable wealth. In his travels through Georgia in 1903, W. E. B. Dubois made note of African American business owners. "Across the way is Gatesby, brown and tall, lord of two thousand acres shrewdly won and held. There is a store conducted by his African American son, a blacksmith shop, and a ginnery" (Adoff, 29-30). As African Americans began to gain an economic, political, and artistic foothold during Reconstruction, White backlash grew. African American prosperity during this period triggered concern throughout White America which sought ways to impede the growth of African American economics. Vincent Harding wrote, in the prologue to *The Eyes on the* Prize, "To dig so deep would reveal to us harsh economic intimidation in the development of a kind of peonage, often called sharecropping. It would recount through much of the 1870s and 1880s the misuses of political, legal, and social systems in a ruthless attempt to deny, subvert, and destroy the power of Blackness that had briefly appeared in the land during Reconstruction" (Carson, et al 5).

The Ku Klux Klan was founded in the 1890s as a reaction against a rising African American working and middle class that was becoming increasingly independent of White America. Martin Luther King Jr.'s father was harassed by the Klan in the 1930s because of his father's increasing prosperity and political influence. Biographer Stephen B. Oates writes about the family's move to the bluffs overlooking downtown Atlanta:

> The new house was a two-story brick dwelling – precisely the kind Daddy had promised to own one day. He was now 'a major force' in Atlanta's Black community, a man with considerable business interests and political and social clout. He belonged to a small interracial coalition and was prominent in the Negro Voters League. Because he was a Negro on the climb, he received abusive letters and phone calls from the Ku Klux Klan. (13-14)

In 1896, through the Supreme Court's decision in the *Plessy* v. *Ferguson* case which ruled that separate facilities for African Americans did not violate the Fourteenth Amendment, Jim Crow laws were introduced and "Separate but Equal" living became the law. White America was afraid of losing its social and economic advantage. Violence against African Americans increased yearly. The National Association for the Advancement of Colored People is a political, economical, educational, and civic organization founded in 1909 that is still active and strong today. The NAACP totaled the number of lynchings, hangings, and murders of African Americans to be more than 100 (a conservative number, certainly) per year by the turn of the century. (Hatch and Shine 61) Federal, state, and local governments were mostly unable or unwilling to stem the tide of blatant crime against African American citizens. The NAACP hired investigators to collect evidence, which was turned over to the government in hopes of convicting lynchers. Walter White wrote an account of his work for the NAACP as an investigator of lynchings and race riots at the turn of the century. His investigations of forty-one lynchings and eight race riots over a decade indicate a remarkable lack of concern on the part of law officials and politicians. White, a fair-skinned, blue-eyed African American man, easily able to "pass" for a White man, was able to interview leading figures of lynch mobs. In 1918 he walked into the store of a man who had led a group of local Whites in the lynching of an African American woman who was pregnant and ten African American men in Georgia. The store owner was guarded until Walter White expressed support for the lynchers.

'You'll pardon me, Mister', he began, 'for seeming suspicious but we have to be careful. In ordinary times we wouldn't have anything to worry about, but with the war there's been some talk of the Federal government looking into lynchings. It seems there's some sort of law during wartime making it treason to lower the man power of the country.'

'In that case I don't blame you for being careful,' I assured him. 'But couldn't the Federal government do something if it wanted to when a lynching takes place, even if no war is going on at the moment?' 'Naw,' he said, confidently, proud of the opportunity of displaying his store of information to one who he assumed know nothing whatever about the subject. 'There's no such law, in spite of all the agitation by a lot of fools who don't know the niggers as we do. States' rights won't permit Congress to meddle in lynching in peace time.' 'But what about your state government—your Governor, your sheriff, your police officers?' 'Humph! Them? We elected them to office, didn't we? And the niggers, we've got them disfranchised, ain't we? Sheriffs and police and Governors and prosecuting attorneys have got too much sense to mix in lynching-bees. If they do they know they might as well give up all idea of running for office any more--if something worse don't happen to them--' (Adoff 36-38).

Violence against African Americans continued to occur unchecked as the century got underway.

Thomas Dixon, a minister, wrote the 1906 novel, *The Clansman*, in Christian defense of the Ku Klux Klan. The novel was made into a play and then a film by D. W. Griffith called *Birth of a Nation*. In the story mobs of Whites become vigilantes in the capture and killing of African American men who are depicted as rapists and raving, dangerous lunatics. The propaganda was meant to place fear in the hearts of White Americans and to justify the continued slaughtering of African Americans.

Against this backdrop of terror African American dramatic writing took on a tone of extreme caution and a deep seated mistrust against White Americans. The bonds that brought slaves and freed men together with White abolitionists prior to emancipation became strained as African American prosperity fostered resentment amongst even liberal Whites. African Americans' rights through Reconstruction began to be tenuous. At this time several schools of thought about what Vincent Harding calls the "post-Reconstruction African American movement toward new freedom and extended equality" were gaining influence. Booker T. Washington, head of the African American college, Tuskegee Institute, began stressing a less confrontational approach to racist America and emphasized the need for the development of a viable skill or trade through advanced education. Garveyism, based on the charismatic leader, Marcus Garvey, called for a defiant return to Africa, the motherland and Zion of his followers. W. E. B. Dubois was an influential political writer whose vision for African America was a blend of Washington's stress on education but with a push for intellectual development and Marcus Garvey's confrontational style of freedom fighting.

Aunt Betsy's Thanksgiving by Katherine D. Chapman Tillman in 1914 reflected the cautious, non-confrontational stance in dealing with Whites espoused by Booker T. Washington. In this short one act play, Nellie, the daughter of Aunt Betsy, ran away from her violent husband one day only to return 12 years later to find her mother and her child, both of whom she had taken for dead, living in a cabin on land that she had purchased. Nellie is afraid to approach her family for fear that White hostility toward her real estate purchase would backfire on her elderly mother. The previous owner was intending to evict Aunt Betsy and 12 year old Caroline. Nellie's secret purchase through a White saves Aunt Betsy from eviction. Nellie sends a letter through a lawyer stating that the property is newly purchased and will be renovated and additionally, Aunt Betsy was to be paid three dollars monthly to live on the premises. The letter is signed by a mysterious Sylvia Dean. Finally, at the close of the play Nellie reveals herself and explains her covert actions.

> Nellie: Mother, forgive me, it was I. I had given
> you up as dead long ago, in fact I had been told that
> you was, and of course I thought Caroline was dead.
> Colonel Everly had given Mr. Rodney some land for a
> school here at Everly. I had worked hard for years for a
> home of my own and I had bought this land through a
> white friend from the North, not knowing that you lived on
> it or lived anywhere on earth. When I saw Caroline that
> day, the truth flashed on my mind, but knowing the
> prejudice against colored people getting good property, by
> the advice of my white friend, Mrs. Sylvia Deane, I went
> away without seeing you until now. I cannot tell you all
> my story now, but I am here to be with you and Caroline
> always. (Hamalian and Hatch 132)

The play is brief and burdened with an overly melodramatic plot based on a set of coincidental circumstances but its poignancy can be seen in the social and political carefulness of its characters. They are far less brash and confident than the characters of the previous generation. And yet, the fearfulness of the time did not keep African Americans from striving forward in business and education or keep dramatists from writing about it.

World War I brought about the enlistment of many African American soldiers. W. E. B. DuBois and other prominent African American leaders initially encouraged African Americans to join the ranks in the fight to protect democracy until the reality of racism on American shores became too hypocritical to bear. DuBois wrote, "They cheat us and mock us; they kill us and slay us; they deride our misery. When we plead for the naked protection of the law ... they tell us to 'GO TO HELL! (Hatch, Hamalian 135). A new and angry reaction was stirring in African Americans. Mary Burrill's 1919 drama *Aftermath*, illustrates the sentiment. Set during World War I, *Aftermath*, tells the story of an African American soldier returning from war. Armed with post-battle aggression and two army pistols, John is sharply contrasted with his friend Lonnie, a civilian. Lonnie is docile and fearful, while John is defiant.

Millie: See what John done brought you! An'
look on de mantel! (*pointing to the pistols*)

Lonnie: (*drawing back in fear as he glances at the pistols*)
You'd bettah hide them things! No cullud man bettah be
seen wid dem things down heah!

John: That's all right, Lonnie, nevah you fear. I'm goin'
to keep 'em an' I ain't a-goin' to hide 'em either. See
them. (*pointing to the wound chevrons on his arm*) Well,
when I got them wounds, I let out all the rabbit-blood 'at
wuz in me! Ef I kin be trusted with a gun in France, I kin
be trusted with one in South Car'lina. (Hamalian and
Hatch 148)

The result of having fought and been wounded in war on foreign soil
made John rebellious against the racial violence that was so prevalent in
America. In the final scene of this one act drama John learns that his father
has been lynched by Whites. Here, the contrast between John and the other
characters is greatest. Lonnie, Mam Sue, and Millie are all desperately
afraid of White violence. When Old man Withrow and the Sherley boys
came to drag his father out of the house, no one tried to stop them.
Furthermore, no one bothered to tell John about the lynching until the end
of the story. They welcome him home from the war without mentioning
the incident. He finds out by accident from a neighbor. This detail gives
the drama and its social implications a macabre twist as we see how a
group of people can become so frightened as to withhold information of
that magnitude. John, as the African American race's voice of rage, heads
out in the end to seek revenge. The revenge is far more than a vendetta,
however. It is a cry for freedom and a protest against post-slavery re-
enslavement.

John: (*bitterly*) I've been helpin' the w'ite man git
his freedom. I reckon I'd bettah try now to get my own!

Mam Sue: (*terrified*) Whut yuh gwine ter do?

John: (*with bitterness growning in his voice*) I'm sick
o' these w'ite folks doin's – "we're 'fine, trus'worthy
feller citizuns" when they're handin' us out guns, an'
Liberty Bonds, , an' chuckin' us off to die; but we ain't
a damn thing when it comes to handin' us the rights we
done fought an' fled fu'! I'm sick o' this sort o' life – an'
I'm goin' to put an' end to it!

Millie: (*rushing to the mantel and covering the revolvers
with her hands*) Oh, no, no, John! Mam Sue, John's
gwine to kill hisse'f!

Mam Sue: Oh, mah honey, don' yuh go do nothin' to bring
sin on yo' soul! Pray to de good Lawd to tek all dis
fiery feelin' out'n yo' heart! Wait 'tel Brudder Moseby
come back – he's gwine to pray –

John: This ain't no time fu' preachers or prayers! You
mean to tell me I mus' let them w'ite devuls send me miles
erway to suffer an' be shot up fu' the freedom of people I
ain't nevah seen while they're burnin' an' killin' my folks
here at home! To Hell with 'em!

Millie: (*throwing her arms about his neck*) Oh, John,
they'll kill yuh!

John: Whut ef they do! I ain't skeered o' none of 'em! I've
faced worse guns than any sneakin' hounds kin show me!
To Hell with 'em! (*he thrusts the revolver that he has
just loaded into* Lonnie's *hand*) Take this, an' come
on here, boy, an' we'll see what Withrow an' his gang
have got to say! (Hamalian and Hatch 150-151)

African American outrage just after the turn of the century was being
countered by the politics of assimilation. James V. Hatch stated, "In this
milieu Booker T. Washington sought ways to prevent the complete social,
political and economic re-enslavement of the Negro people. His   method

was not militancy but accommodation. He assured White southerners that 'Your families will be surrounded by the most patient, faithful, law-abiding and un-resentful people that the world has seen" (Hatch 61). Intra-cultural protest was direct and self-indicting. Joseph S. Cotter, Sr.'s 1901 play, *Caleb the Degenerate*, rebuked the anti-establishment sentiments of African Americans who might engage in the practices of smoking, drinking, lying, stealing, or drug use and turn to Christian values as practiced by "good negroes." These values included learning a trade, saving money, and refraining from any involvement with African American militant movements like Garveyism. Cotter wrote the following preface to his play:

> The Negro needs very little politics, much industrial training, and a dogged settledness as far as going to Africa is concerned. To this should be added clean, intelligent fireside leadership. Much of any other kind is dangerous for the present. I am a Negro and speak from experience. (Hatch 63)

Caleb, the central character, is depicted one-dimensionally as a self-destructive brute who dies by his own self-inflicted wounds just after repenting before God and the Bishop. His sins are conveniently blamed on his heritage, allowing his social conditions and the effects of racism in White America to escape culpability.

> Doctor: . . . His mother sinned ere he was born.
> This tainted him, therefore his wicked course.
>
> Caleb: O, God, if I have sinned because the blood
> Thou gavest me was tainted ere my birth,
> Whose is the wrong? Whose is the reckoning?
> Master I leave it all with Thee – with Thee. (Hatch 95)

Caleb, like Aaron in *Titus Andronicus*, is arrogantly individualistic and critical of the status quo. His wanton behavior is a reaction against what he considers the hypocritical and shallow morals of would-be Christians.

Caleb: Patsy, Your husband has it in his pauper breast.
He boasted of a hide-bound honesty.
I boast me of my liberty and wit.

Bishop: You are a monster!

Caleb: You have spoken truth!

Bishop: You know not God!

Caleb: You mean God knows not me!

Bishop: You are an infidel?

Caleb: I am! I am!

Bishop: You move without a current, sail, or creed!

Caleb: My current is myself! My wit's my sail!

Bishop: Your creed?

Caleb: I have a creed! It suits you not!

Bishop: What is it?

Caleb: Here it is! Prepare your ire!
Men stagger in my light, yet are too dull
To see that my creed is infallible,
They rather worship God whose cruel laws
Are made up wholly of mistakes and flaws.
The time shall be when they will cease to follow
Views that are so disgusting and so hollow. (Hatch 70)

Caleb's mockery of the church and his savagery are displayed as indisputably base, particularly in contrast with the Bishop and his daughter who run the trade school for African Americans. In this superficial treatment we can see how Cotter attempted to protest the adherence to the principles of the angry African American separatist who would follow the "Back to Africa" teachings of Marcus Garvey rather than be religiously fervent and industrious in a trade of labor. Hatch states, "Yes, Mr.Cotter is urging the African American man to follow Dr. Washington's work ethic. As has been suggested, the race virulence of America was at a crest in Cotter's time. Solutions for survival had to be found. Yes, the play was written with an eye to the white reader" (62). Cotter sought to reassure White America that a cooperative African American race could adhere to the values prescribed by Whites. Further, he sought to reassure White America that they were not to blame for the despairing lives of African Americans. Consequently, the drama was praised by Whites. The play was sent to English poet laureate, Alfred Austin, who responded with, "It affords yet further evidence of the latent capacity of your long maltreated race for mental development" (Hatch 62). Author Israel Zangwill commented, ". . . I desire to express my appreciation of the passages of true poetry in which you express the aspirations of the Negro race for salvation by labor" (Hatch 62).

The Golden Age and the Harlem Renaissance

The "Golden Age" of African Americans in theatre is marked by a collectivism that is evident in the rise of theatre companies rather than in a proliferation of dramatic writings. The period roughly spans from the 1909 with the first Harlem theatre movement until the explosive Harlem Renaissance period of 1921. The term "Afro-American" is first used in this era. The first Harlem theatre, the Crescent, was established by two White businessmen who turned the theatre over to a tenacious African American manager named Eddie Hunter in 1909. Harlem became New York City's first suburb in the late 19th century. Prior to that period Harlem was primarily an area populated with corrugated huts and an occasional fashionable home – notably the home of Alexander Hamilton. By 1886 three overhead subway lines were built that extended to Harlem and New York's elite began to spread north where elaborate mansions and brownstone buildings were erected. Shortly after the turn of the century African Americans began to flood Harlem through a real estate miscalculation. Developers had built on every available vacant lot but were unable to rent the homes that were too highly priced for the average foreigner living in New York City (Mitchell, 28). Realtors found that they could get away with charging African Americans much higher rents, and so the influx began. Many wealthy Whites living in the area fled further north. As African Americans settled into Harlem, the arts began to grow. Leonard C. Archer stated, "All elements of the Black theatre were together for the first time in the Harlem theatres – actors, writers, musicians, dancers, and producers. This Harlem interlude brought into being the all-Black musical comedy, all-Black vaudeville circuit and road companies, the Harlem night club theatres and legitimate theatre" (11). Had White downtown theatres permitted African American practitioners to participate in its ventures, the Harlem Golden Age and the Renaissance might not have been such a tour de force. African Americans were determined to engage in artistic expression – with or without the aid of White America. Archer further asserted, "Segregation and discrimination, based on race and color, brought about wider separation of native cultures between Negroes and whites and promoted a spirit of Negro nationalism . . . Inspired by this spirit of national independence, the Black performers lifted themselves by their own bootstraps" (13).

In addition to the Crescent theatre on 135th Street, the Lincoln, the Lafayette, which is now the New Lafayette Theatre headed by Woodie King, Jr., and the Alhambra were founded.

Writer-actor-producer Eddie Hunter ran the Crescent theatre where seven and sometimes eight daily stock shows and comedy sketches ran between three to six weeks. Hunter and other African American performers were making the transition from vaudeville and beginning to act without blackface makeup.

> Once a discussion came up about Black comedians putting burnt cork on their faces. I said: 'Let me tell you something: I don't need cork to be funny. It is just what they are doing these days, so I put it on. . . . A bet came up about that and I said I'd do a sketch in which I wouldn't use cork. I decided to write a sketch called *The Gentleman Burglar* [. . .]. (Mitchell 51)

The Gentleman Burglar was not a sketch that particularly bolstered the African American identity but it highlights the fact that African

Americans were beginning to commandeer their own venues and move away from White theatrical aesthetics, which was a significant achievement. In an interview with Loften Mitchell in the 1960s, Eddie Hunter shared his belief, " . . . that what has retarded the Harlem theatre movement is the attempt of 'middle-class' Negroes to be just like white folks" (Mitchell 67).

The most well-known and most important early African American theatre group was The Lafayette Players founded in 1915 by Anita Bush, a chorus girl turned theatre manager. The Lafayette Theatre building was first leased by Martinson and Niber, the two White businessmen who first employed Eddie Hunter to run the Crescent. The company staged *Darktown Follies, Servant in the House,* and *Justice* in addition to standard Broadway shows. In explaining the production of Broadway shows, Archer quotes James Weldon Johnson as saying, " . . . the Negro found himself free of a great many restraints and taboos in these plays" (12). Fabre criticized the practice, stating, "Surprisingly, the emerging Black theatre gave little attention to the Black community and to the development of a cultural politics on its behalf. If one defines Black theatre as a theatre about Blacks, written by Blacks, and acted by Blacks for a Black audience, then only the first of these conditions was satisfied" (7). In truth, the Lafayette Theatre, as well as the Lincoln Theatre was well-supported by the African American community to the extent that the Lafayette Players were compelled by the community to support its people by people like Lovett Fort-Whiteman, the drama editor of the African American newspaper, *The Messenger.* In an article written in 1917, Fort Whiteman demanded that the company desist from staging White dramas and produce plays that reflected the lives of African Americans so that, "our society be reflected upon the American stage even if we have to call a mass meeting of Harlem's theatergoers and effect a boycott on the Lafayette Theatre" (30). The Lafayette Players sent out a prize-awarding request for original African American plays which rendered poor results (Hill 3). The writing of African American drama did not fully re-emerge from the late 19th century until the Harlem Renaissance in 1920. The period of White retaliation against African Americans between the late 1800s and the early 1900s sent many pro-African American dramatists underground. But African American writers and performers of the early 20th century were also insecurely on a mission to prove to White Americans that they could compete on the same playing field. The attempt to assimilate and gain notice from Whites in theatre and in society during this period was great. David Krasner explains this as the "double consciousness" of Blacks (8).

He describes the phenomenon as such:

> Black theatre from 1895 to 1910 was marked by both a resistance to the caricatures created by white "blackface" minstrelsy, and a resistance to Jim Crowism, lynching, and racist pseudo-science. However, theatrical resistance to racism during the late nineteenth and first decades of the twentieth century was, in general, neither an overt act of confrontation nor an admixture of revolutionary dogman, but rather a gradual movement, a phenomenon of advances and retreats. Resistance was often combined with an *appearance of accommodation;* attitudes of adjustment enabled Black Americans to survive in the American caste system during the turn of the century. (5)

Indeed, Many African American performers made great efforts to be part of the downtown Broadway scene. Exile from mainstream theatre sent African American practitioners north to perform works that they hoped would gain the attention of downtown Whites. However, changes in American consciousness, namely a sense of national pride, were also taking place in African American awareness, as well.

Between 1917 and 1929 America moved into a period of dramatic nationalism, rejecting the European standards that had been so prevalent in the staging and writing of plays. European classics were being replaced by American themes and characters in plays like Eugene O'Neill's *The Hairy Ape* and Elmer Rice's *The Adding Machine*. The "little theatre" movement, spearheaded by groups like the Provincetown Players, were concerned with promoting American playwriting.

In Harlem, where the population increased from 50,000 in 1914 to 200,000 by 1930, an African American nationalism, similar to the widespread American nationalism was taking place. The era of "Negro Folk" drama and heroes had begun. Alain Locke, a leading African American scholar, spokesman for the African American theatre movement, and professor of philosophy at Howard University in Washington D.C., "saw the need for experimentation in form and urged on Black theatre artists the courage to be original, to break with established dramatic convention of all sorts and develop their own idiom"(Hill 5). Locke and Professor Montgomery Gregory established the first theatre department at the all-African American institution. He felt that African American folk art and folk heroes were critical to the development of African American theatre without the superimposition of White American theatre conventions and aesthetics. Locke further proposed the idea that "One can scarcely think of a complete development of Negro dramatic art without some significant artistic expression of African American life and the traditions associated with it" (Hill 5). The NAACP formed the first theatre company that was strictly devoted to the ideology of Alain Locke. Their theatrical group, established in 1928 was called the Krigwa Players. The group operated out of the basement of the 135th street Harlem Library with the sole purpose of presenting African American plays for African American audiences with a non-separatist approach that welcomed all races through its doors. The growth of African American companies continued throughout the Harlem Renaissance period and groups like the Ethiopian Art Players, the Negro Art Theatre, and the Harlem Community Players embracing African and African American ideology. Outside of Harlem, similar companies were forming. In Cleveland, the Karamu Theatre was started by the Lafayette Players. In Washington D.C. the Howard Players from Howard University were performing *The Death Dance* (1923) by Thelma Duncan and *Sadhji* (1927) by Richard Bruce, both plays being set in African villages.

Throughout the 1930s efforts toward building African American theatres, establishing a permanent Negro theatre and increasing African American drama and patronage continued. Actor, director, and theatre builder Dick Campbell was a leading figure in the push for dignified drama by and about African Americans. He was against such plays as Marc Connelly's *Green Pastures* which won the 1930 Pulitzer Prize, because he felt it was a distorted view of African America as seen through the lens of White sentimentality. Campbell, along with Rose McClendon, a talented actress, started the Negro Peoples Theatre in 1935. Ironically, the company opened with a well-received African American version of *Waiting for Lefty* that was its only production. Rose McClendon died and Campbell became the head of the Negro Unit of the Federal Theatre later that year. In 1939 Campbell and his singer-actress wife, Muriel Rahn, opened the Rose McClendon Players which became the most influential African American theatre of its day. The Rose McClendon players became a company that provided theatre training for its members through the Moscow Art Players. Langston Hughes opened the Harlem Suitcase Theatre in 1938 with a group of performers.

For the first time in history a balance was created between the growth in companies and the dramatic writing of African Americans. Throughout the 1940s the call for an African American ideology in the arts and society grew stronger. The 1940s left behind the gentility of middle class African American ethics of the early 19th century and the Negro folk drama of the 1920s and 30s. Goodman states, "With such writers as Richard Wright, Melvin Tolson, William Attaway, Robert Hayden, Gwendolyn Brooks, Ralph Ellison, and James Baldwin, the protest tradition continued in varying degrees through the forties and fifties and culminated in the shrill demands and vituperations of those Black writers involved in the Black revolution of the sixties" (23). Richard Wright's character, Bigger Thomas, in the 1941 play, *Native Son*, epitomizes the new social protest of the period. He is the angry, violent embodiment of inner city rage that marked the birth of civil rights actions in America. The Broadway version was "softened" so as to be palatable for White audiences but the tradition of protest was carried on in dramas such as Dorothy Heyward's 1948 *Set My People Free*, and through the efforts of companies like the American Negro Theatre established in 1940. Loften Mitchell described the impact of the American Negro Theatre on the African American theatre movement thus:

> There was a great social revolution underway, the plays of protest, the plays of social meaning, and this was the kind of theatre were trying to develop. Not just for entertainment and our own professional growth and artistry, but we wanted to say something significant and meaningful to the people . . . . We were a people's theatre. (147)

The Cold War rampaged the United States in the 1950s and African American theatrical productivity was impacted as were all arts in America. The "fearful fifties" with its anti-communist hysteria made protest a dangerous endeavor. African American politics in writing and onstage were labeled subversive and many liberal White patrons of the arts distanced themselves from African American theatrical activity. This began an era of African American backlash against White liberals who were attacked by writers like James Baldwin and artists like Leroi Jones. The government's subpoenas of artists who were accused of being engaged in un-American activities took its toll on African American theatre companies. Internal clashes and defections left many companies floundering. There was little work for African American actors and the dramatic offerings of the 1950s were bland and non-controversial. Lorraine Hansberry's 1959 family drama, *A Raisin in the Sun*, symbolized the era of the "nots"; plays not about African Americans or propaganda; plays not designed to make White America uncomfortable. Gerald Goodman states, "The kind of play that Broadway would accept in the fifties is exemplified by *A Raisin in the Sun*" (132).

In 1950 the Council on the Harlem Theatre was created to examine new directions for African American theatre. Their specific purpose was three-fold: 1) to establish support through a networking between the companies that would provide a sharing of assets – namely, actors, scenery, and mailing lists; 2) to coordinate production calendars so the various groups would not be in competition with one another for audiences; and 3) to agitate for more truthful African American plays. In 1951 the Committee for Negroes in the Arts was formed with the intention of producing more reactionary drama. Goodman contends, "For the most part, Black playwrights of the fifties quietly and without bitterness affirmed the need for justice, tolerance and understanding between Black and white Americans" (124).

In the midst of the turmoil between unrealistic African American drama and the call for more realistic, confrontational drama, the Greenwich Mews Theatre produced a series of integrated offerings and formally introduced the concept and practice of color blind casting. The theatre, housed in the basement of the Village Presbyterian Church and the Brotherhood Synagogue in 1952 produced Shaw's *Widower's Houses* and Les Pine's *Monday's Heroes*. The idea of casting a play without regard to color or race unless otherwise specified was considered novel and timely during the nation's strive for integration by its proponents. Its detractors felt that the practice would ultimately end in the de-culturalization and dehumanization of the African American race. This is where the argument commences.

From the forced merger and systematic sublimation of African American culture in early colonial America to the beginning of the formal debate on cross-racial casting African Americans have overwhelmingly striven for self - assertion. It has been a reactionary declaration trailing behind the racial politics in America, but one that has employed every opportunity to present itself as a legitimate culture and art worthy of equal footing in American society. Krasner affirms, "I will argue that the aesthetics of Black modernism arose from resistance to racism on the one hand, and a need for social integration and cooperation among Black Americans on the other" (4-5). Critical to the overview is the fact that despite society's systematic attempts to obliterate an African/African American self-image, African American drama developed an identity independent of White American indoctrination. The earliest companies in the first half of the 19th century presented classics as they experimented with American/European strategies. In the mid- to late 19th century dramas about African American life and social protest were staged. As an African American aesthetic became more articulated its drama branched into various forms of intra-cultural and intercultural communication. African American theatre artists have fought valiantly to establish and preserve their identities and experiences onstage. It is this 200 year old struggle that provides the rationale for assessing the practice of color-blind casting. This historical overview is presented to demonstrate the drive toward establishing an African American cultural/theatrical identity since the beginning of slavery and throughout subsequent eras until the period when color blind casting practices formally came into question. The following chapter explores the socio-psychological identity formations of African Americans that are basis of the need for African American particularism in theatre.

Chapter Four

AFRICAN AMERICAN SOCIAL IDENTITY FORMATION
IN AMERICA

Chapter Three of this study revealed the formation of an African American identity in theatre and the drive to form new identities in drama over a 200 year period. This chapter on race and identity-making provides insight into how and why the socio-psychological process of identity-formation has occurred historically within the general body of African American people. Chapter Three intersects with this chapter in that it explores an expression of African American identity – drama, ritual, and performance -- and much of the historical evidence overlaps. Yet it is distinguishable from the socio-behavioral aspects of race and identity-making as an external feature of identity rather than an internal feature. Both cultural and psychological development combine to produce a total identity. Here, key revelations about the socio-behavioral developmental process can proffer a practical understanding of the push for the formation of a clear African American identity and the general needs and aims of theatre for African Americans. This would, in the final analysis (the concluding chapter), assist in determining whether colorblind casting practices conjoin with the general aspirations of this particular ethnic group. Herein lies the methodology for ultimately determining the effects of color blind casting on African American theatre and society. It is necessary to delineate between the identity-formation of the early years (in this chapter) and the identity politics of the later years (discussed in Chapters One and Two) because, as Orlando Patterson, Harvard sociology professor states, "Identity politics took its modern form during the second half of the last century. It emerged as an emancipatory mode of political action and thinking based on the shared experience of injustice by particular groups – notably Blacks, women, gays, Latinos and American Indians" (2).

The purpose in focusing this chapter on the period from the initial captivity of Africans to the advent of African American psychology in the mid 20th century is twofold: a) to identify this span of time as the evolvement of a uniquely African American identity reformulated from

African and American influences; and   b) to pinpoint the direction of the development of African American race identity up till the mid 20th century.

At this juncture, discourse about the fundamentals of self-conception and the prototype for identity-making will provide the basis for understanding how and why African American distinctiveness figures in the question of color-blind casting in Chapter Five. A definition of key terms is necessary to comprehend the psychological processes that create identity. The connection between those terms and how they figure in the development of African American culture will follow. This chapter will conclude with further insights on the psychological findings on African American cultural needs and the fulfillment of those needs in society.

This study draws upon the key concepts of self-identity (subsuming identification and re-identification), self-concept, self-esteem, group identity, including social identity theory, to assess the internal needs of the African American population. These concepts can be cross-referenced to any group – religious, ethnic, social, etc. – however, in this study they are applied specifically to African American psychology. Modern Black psychology is a relatively recent development of the late 1960s which addresses the unique socio-psychological processes of identity-making within that group. Leaders in the field at that time, such as Joseph L. White, Thomas A. Parham, and Adelbert H. Jenkins, had sought to build conceptual models of behavior based on an African American cultural view. Wayne State sociology professor, Richard L. Allen quotes scholars Markus' and Kitayama's assertion that the "European-American view of the self and its relation to the collective is only *one* view. There are other, equally powerful but strikingly different, collective notions about the self and its relation to the collective" (46). This chapter intends to outline the basic socio-psychological dynamics of identity formation using one set of social and behavioral theories applied to the above socio-psychological terms. The examination of social and behavioral theory forms the groundwork upon which the development of an African American identity may be evaluated but by no means exhausts the topic. In this chapter the focus will be on the period of the need to cultivate such an identity and the thrust toward identity-making.

To begin, "self-identity," or as Allen terms, "personal identity," addresses one's individual characteristics (49).   Sociologist Jean S. Phinney applies her findings, called social identity theory, to the concept of self-identity, which asserts that people instinctively endeavor to advance their sense of self and that individuals discover self, in large part, through others (499-501). The Zulu expression of this idea is called *umuntu umuntu ngabantu* which means "a person is a person through other people" (Allen 47). Essentially, we, as individuals, wish for and strive to feel positive about ourselves. Further, we seek affirmation in our larger macrocosms to enhance our self-identity. Thus, the development of positive self-identity follows a two-part process of internal self-characterization and self-characterization as reflected through external effects. Further, internal and external effects are mutually dependent in the formation of self-identity.

In Talmadge Anderson's research, identification is commonly defined by behavioral theorists as " . . . a psychological phenomenon that serves to increase the feelings of worth and importance by identifying with, or taking on the characteristics, values, or cultural attributes of some person or group that is well received by others" (Azibo 21). Identification is the process whereby individuals form a self-identity. Anderson goes on to state that identification is psychologically essential for the ego development and maintenance of the individual or group (21). Re-identification, then, is the psychological process of reforming identity from initial identification into something dissimilar. Re-identification is neither a negative or positive occurrence. The quality of the new identity that has been fashioned determines whether negative or positive psychological conditions will result.

Another term, "self-concept," has posed definitional problems for behavioral scientists. Allen states, ". . . imprecision, inattention to definitional boundaries, and interchangeability of terms have characterized this use. It is not uncommon for several different concept names to be used to express the one notion of self or of the self-concept. Careful explication of the self-concept is rare. As a consequence, confusion abounds. . ." (50). Indeed, the term "self-concept" is often interchanged with self-identity. Allen, whose definition will be used throughout this chapter, has found it useful to distinguish the terms by placing self-identity as a component at the center of self-conception, meaning that the formation of self-identity, both internally and externally, creates one's self-concept.

Global assumptions have been made concerning the nature of the self-concept, which Allen outlines as follows:

1.   The self-concept is the cognitive component of the psychological process known as the self.
2.   Individuals possess many self-concepts.

3.   The self-concept is situation specific. That is, self-concepts tend to operate in specific situations producing particular self-conceptions.

4.   The self-concept is a highly complex, evolving entity, offering different components of its totality for investigation. (126)

Point two, which addresses the multi-faceted aspect of self-conception, and point four, which asserts a fluid, ever-developing self-conception will be most useful to this segment of the study.

"Self-esteem," another term to be included in this chapter, is also rarely defined in satisfactory scientific terms. It is often presumed to be self-explanatory and scholars discuss the term as if it embodied universally accepted meanings. Self-esteem is described by Allen as a basic human motive (48). Allen goes on to posit, ". . . humans possess an insatiable desire to protect and refine their feeling of self-worth" (48). He addresses the characteristics of self-esteem without defining the term. Anderson discusses self-esteem in terms of levels and the influence of self-actualization and racial identity but never actually defines the concept either. James Haskins and Hugh F. Butts, M.D., never define the main variable in their studies on skin-color perception and self-esteem. They credit racial oppression as a factor in lowering self-esteem and measure self-esteem through the California Test of Personality (C.T.P.), but never elucidate on the nature of this phenomenon. Likewise, Joseph L. White, in *The Psychology of Blacks: An Afro-American Perspective*, examines the self-esteem of African American children without providing a working definition of the term. Morris Rosenberg, author of *Self-Concept Research: A Historical Overview*, offered a simple, yet succinct definition of self-esteem as ". . . generalized feelings of self-worth or self-acceptance" (36). It is critical in any study of identity-forming to be able to employ a comprehensible model of self-esteem to determine whether it is a necessary component of self-concept. Webster's New World Dictionary provides a working definition similar to Rosenberg's. Webster's states that self-esteem is:

n. 1. belief in oneself; self-respect. 2. undue pride in oneself. (1322)

The first definition, pertaining to self-respect, is the concept that social behaviorists and psychologists generally refer to when discussing identity-making processes. Belief in oneself and a sense of self-respect, according to Allen, is an intrinsic human value that we seek to enhance throughout life (48). Allen goes on to splinter the term into several principles--two of which are most applicable to this study--whereby self-esteem is developed. The first, reflective appraisal, is the concept that individuals' feelings about themselves tend to be predicated upon what others/society feel about them. With respect to self-esteem, feelings of self-worth are strongly influenced by the worth accorded us by social others, including family, peers, and society at large.

Similar to reflective appraisal, the second principle, social comparison, rests upon social interaction wherein society is a significant point of reference. Social comparison " . . . contends that given no objective information about self, the person judges himself or herself based on comparisons with relevant others" (Allen 48). Social comparison differs from reflective appraisal in that there is a distinct absence of self-reflective mechanisms, requiring the individual to substitute external images and views for internal constructs.

Social identity theory, according to Allen, presupposes the notion that people strive for a positive sense of self and make considerable efforts to enhance and protect self-concept (49). Allen further elucidates the theory by placing "group identity," a major consideration in this chapter, and "personal identity" as sub-features of social identity. Personal identity refers to one's individual characteristics while group identity refers to the characteristics of one's group. Personal and group identity are compoundingly related. Personal identity pertains to self-esteem, self-concept, self-identification, self-worth, and a myriad of other terms that reflect an individual's view of him or herself.

"Group identity" carries considerable weight in the formation of a positive personal identity. Phinney's 1990 article for the *Psychological Bulletin* titled "Ethnic Identity in Adolescents and Adults" argues that an individual's attitudes toward his primary reference group are greatly connected to that individual's psychological well-being. Phinney mentions the particular importance of this connection for members of culturally, economically, and politically disenfranchised groups. Allen states that a number of scholars are in unanimous agreement with this theory of the importance of group identity as a means toward maintaining a strong degree of self-worth.

"Group identity" in African American psychology is another term that has posed definitional problems for behavioral scientists. It has been alternately labeled reference group orientation, ethnic identity, racial identity, global self-esteem, race esteem, and racial self-identification, among other terms. Phinney has provided a clear definition, using the term "ethnic identity" rather than group identity, as being "an aspect of an individual's self-concept that stems from knowledge of his or her membership in a group and the significance attached to that membership, the sense of shared values and attitudes, and the awareness of behaviors, values, and history of the group" (200-201).

As revealed earlier, personal identity and group identity are mutually dependent. Anderson confers that, "A person normally has a related individual [personal] and collective [group] identity" (21). Anderson goes on to argue that sometimes the personal and the group identity of an individual are in conflict which can lead to psychological disorder or misorientation.

Where and how does race factor into this discussion on identity-making? Ralph Ellison, author of *The Invisible Man* stated, "When I discover who I am, I'll be free." The implication here is that knowing self leads to an appreciation of and a development of a positive self-concept. It is also safe to assert from the previously mentioned social/behavioral theories that knowing self requires knowledge of self individually and in the context of group identity. So, African Americans must consider who they are individually and as members of a greater collective. Historically, this has not been an easy task. Given what drama theorist David Krasner and many social theorists label the "double-consciousness" of African Americans, unraveling identity can be problematic. Double-consciousness is the phenomenon that occurs when a cultural group has, by choice or force, a split adherence to its own racial identity and another conflicting, dominant racial identity. Double-consciousness is a state of conflict. Identity can become skewed under the converging cultural forces.

The next segment of this chapter will discuss the behavioral concepts and theories in the context of the earliest and greatest identity-forming period of African American existence in America – slavery. The focus on this period is most critical not only because it is the beginning of African American identity formation when African conjoins with American culture but also because it is the period that set in motion the ongoing struggle to gain a high functioning self-identity using African American culture as a primary referent. Leading African American scholar Cornel West explains the inseparableness of history and identity by stating:

> What is particularly naïve and peculiarly vicious about the
> conservative behavioral outlook is that it tends to deny the
> lingering effect of African history—a history inseparable
> from though not reducible to victimization. In this way,
> crucial and indispensable themes of self-help and personal
> responsibility are wrenched out of historical context and
> contemporary circumstances—as if it is all a matter of
> personal will. (14)

In other words, we must look to the roots of the crisis in history to understand African American identity, to build and shore up self-identity for African Americans so as to determine future courses to be taken -- in theatre and society.

Using Phinney's theory of social identity to understand African American self-identity, we can see how the struggle to establish and maintain a clear identity has been challenging. The social identity theory purports that self-identity is formed greatly through one's primary reference group. As mentioned in Chapter Three, African identity was systematically obliterated from the time that newly acquired slaves boarded the boats for American shores. These identity alterations occurred on a psychological level and on a physical level. Allen, in his study of African American identity and self-esteem concurs, stating, "The slave system was both psychological and physical" (18).

This is not to say that all vestiges of African identity were lost. To the contrary, there is much evidence to support the idea that crucial cultural influences were retained over the centuries through oral traditions and concealed practices and that a strong sense of ethnic pride has been cultivated and nurtured in many African Americans; a topic which will be visited in further detail later in this chapter. However, physical survival for African Americans rested upon successful assimilation and adoption of White American ideals as well as denunciation of African/African American culture. Belief in White supremacy was overpoweringly pervasive throughout slavery and post-emancipation times. Abraham Lincoln who was responsible for the Emancipation Proclamation asserted:

> There is a physical difference between the white and black
> races which I believe will forever forbid the two races
> living together on terms of social and political equality,

and inasmuch as they cannot so live, while they do remain together there must be the position of superior and inferior, and I as much as any other man am in favor of having the superior position assigned to the white race. (Sinkler 47).

Thomas Jefferson stated:

I advance it, therefore, as a suspicion only, that the blacks, whether originally a distinct race or made distinct by time and circumstances, are inferior to the Whites in the endowment of both body and mind (Gossett 44).

In 1761 the famous geographer Hallett reduced the entire population of Africa, animals and humans, to a single savage and depraved unit:

It is true that the centre of the continent [Africa] is filled with burning sands, savage beasts and almost uninhabited deserts. The scarcity of water forces the different animals to come together to the same place to drink. It happens that finding themselves together at a time when they are in heat, they have intercourse one with another, without paying regard to the difference between species. Thus, are produced those monsters which are to be found there in greater numbers than in any other part of the world. (Harris 19)

Louis Agassiz, renowned naturalist, reinforced Hallett's views a century later when he wrote:

This compact continent of Africa exhibits a population which has been in example of the Egyptian civilization, of the Phoenician civilization, of the Roman civilization, of the Arab civilization . . . and nevertheless there has never been a regulated society of African men developed on the continent. (Harris 144)

These pervasive sentiments were a later development of the new world resulting after colonialism. Basil Davidson, author of *The African Slave Trade: Precolonial History, 1450-1850* (1961) provides evidence to support the fact that in the 16th century race relations between Europe and Africa were, as often as not, mutually respectful and productive, supported by a healthy, mutual interest. He states, "In the early days of discovery, men in Europe believed they had found partners and allies and equals in Africa" (6). He quotes Ramusio, secretary to the rulers of Venice, who urged the merchants of Italy in 1563 to "Let them go and do business with the King of Timbuktu and Mali . . . and there is no doubt they will be well received there with their ships and their goods, and treated well, and granted the favours that they ask. . . ." (6). Davidson goes on to state, "And if European attitudes toward Africans in those early times displayed a wide range of contrast, they were generally uniform in one important respect. They supposed no natural inferiority in Africans, no inherent failure to develop and mature. That was to be the great myth of later years . . ." (5).

According to Davidson -- and there is overwhelming evidence in support of his claims -- racism is a movement that grew out of the capitalistic mass slave trade ventures. By the height of the trade, attitudes toward Africans and African Americans were generally uniform in the respect of a supposed natural inferiority – quite different from the previous three centuries of race relations. As Abraham Lincoln remarked:

> Negro equality, Fudge! How long, in the government of a God great enough to make and rule the universe shall there continue knaves to vend and fools to quip, so low a piece of demogogism as this. (Sinkler 47)

With leading citizens like United States presidents, world renowned historians, geographers, naturalists, philosophers, and statesmen proclaiming the inferiority of the African race, there is no doubt that forming a positive, proud identity using themselves as a primary referent group would have had less than positive results. The nation, as a whole, including many African Americans, came to see the race as an undesirable population in every aspect of existence. Many slaves came to see the extreme conditions they lived under, the severe treatment they received, and the lowest class of citizenship to be fair, normal, and deserving.

Because Whites believed this to be so, they only had to convince African Americans of those beliefs so that all subscribed to the same ideals. In *American Slave: A Composite Biography*, ex-slave James Johnson related:

> De black man is natchally lazy, you knows dat. A nigger wants what is in sight and not dat what he can't see . . . (43)

Ex-slave Adeline Johnson reminisced:

> I don't set myself up to judge Marse Able Lincoln. Dere is sinners, black and white, but I hope and prays to get to hebben. I wants to be in hebben wid all my white folks, just to wait on them, and love them and serve them, sorta lak I did in slavery time. Dat will be 'nough hebben for Adeline (38-39).

Ex-slave Henry D. Jenkins remembered:

> Yes sir, I doesn't deny it, I got many whuppins. You bet yo' life, my white folks was de bestest in de land. They wasn't mealy mouthed; they make everybody work, sun to sun, seven days in de week. But didn't de good Lord set de 'xample? Yes sir, he made us all work; women in de perils of child birth, drapped cotton seed and corn kernels (24).

Religion is possibly the most influential cultural change imposed upon African America. Theater scholar Femi Euba maintains, " . . . one of the common effects of the impact of European civilization upon African civilization is the conditioning of African religion by Christianity . . ." (10). The act of religious re-identification had such a great impact on

African America. According to Knowles, "The Catholic Church in the West Indies was typically much less hostile and repressive than the Protestant Church on the American mainland. Protestants generally tried to eradicate African rites and rituals when Christianizing the slaves" (28). In over 300 firsthand stories of slavery, approximately 98% mentioned involvement in a church, a relationship with Jesus Christ, or a desire to go to heaven. All slaves in the United States were compelled to recognize Christianity although in some cases they were not permitted to practice the religion. A number of slaveowners forbade slaves to attend White churches, erect their own churches, or gather informally for religious purposes for fear of insurrection. Forbiddance also carried the message that Whites believed African Americans were not worthy of a relationship with their Christian God even while holding them accountable to the tenets of Christianity. Some slave accounts revealed that religion was often encouraged and sometimes mandated on plantations that allowed either attendance in the rear pews of White churches or the building of modest African American churches.

> Mistress was mighty 'ticular 'bout our 'ligion, 'cause she knowed dere was no nigger any too good nohow. Us slaves 'sorbed all de good us had in us from our mistress, I really believes . . .Us was 'bliged to love her, 'cause she knowed us more better than us knowed ourselves. Walter Long. (Rawick 119)

Whether White American Christian practice was denied or demanded by slaveowners the critical issue is that it was the only allowable ritual/spiritual expression. This forced African Americans to discard vital aspects of individual and group identity. Christian practices are far removed from the spiritual practices of African nations. African ceremonies, festivals, and religious observances paid homage to deities like Ogun, Esu-Elegbara, and Anansi, of the Yoruba tradition who represent human qualities. Rituals were dramatic, although, Euba points out that there is still extensive debate "about whether ritual can be called drama" (4) The significant variation lies in the role that religion plays in African culture. Religion is an integral part of African traditions that is at the hub of existence while western Christian religion is compartmentalized by physical space and time. As Euba states, "For traditional [African] religion is inseparable from its culture" (10). Another significant variation between the two religious cultures lies in the physical practices. The dramatic nature of African ritual involves invocation, possession (as in the soul-transportation of modern day Pentecostalism), dance, song, and costuming. Southern American fundamentalist Protestantism during the years of slavery was quite alarmed by the physical and vocal explosiveness of African American practices and saw fit to prohibit any act that did not fit the decorum of dignified Christian religious observances. It is probable that Southerners did not recognize the activities of the slaves as being religious practices at all, when, in fact, African religious, celebratory, and mourning rituals were of the same performance nature. In Knowles' estimation, "Almost every aspect of African life was somehow related to dancing. African people danced in celebration and in mourning, during marriage and initiation rites, in preparation for war, to insure a good hunt and a profitable harvest, for healing, and to make social statements. . . Through the subtlety of their movements, dancers could address social and religious issues, and express gratitude, friendship, or hostility" (22).

Arrival in America meant reforming self-identity to correspond with the identity imposed upon Africans by White America. Over time the new identity became self-imposed and self-regulated and was the basis of a self-concept that was fed by the prevailing Anglo/European influences of that milieu. African Americans had to, essentially, subordinate their natural primary referent group that was threatened in America and adopt an alternate primary referent group, which would support their new identity. Hence, for African Americans in general, their own race became a secondary referent group.

Psychological alterations to identity were reinforced through physical, external alterations of identity. Slaves were made to adopt the dress, dance, religion, language, names, food, music, and all the facets that amount to custom, of European-influenced America. In discussing the Middle Passage, the name given the long journey by ship from Africa to the Americas and the West Indies with newly acquired African captives, Knowles, author of *Tap Roots*, states, "Africans were kidnapped from their homeland and taken to a new environment where they were humiliated, beaten, and dehumanized. Every attempt was made to strip the slaves of their artistic and cultural traditions" (26).

In a circuitous pattern, the number of physical alterations to African culture such as loss of cultural dress that took place ultimately led back to psychological alterations. Before captives boarded the ships for the Middle Passage, all garments, jewelry, and tribal body paintings were removed. Arrival in America subjugated the once kaleidoscopic assemblage of nations into a mono-cultural bastardized reflection of American society. Slave cargo arrived naked. The slave auction blocks sometimes held naked new arrivals and sometimes bore already seasoned slaves dressed in the European-influenced American attire as in the case of Louisiana slave Solomon Northrup:

> In the first place we were required to wash thoroughly, and those with beards to shave. We were then furnished with a new suit each, cheap, but clean. The men had hat, coat, shirt, pants and shoes; the women frocks of calico, and handkerchief to bind about their heads. (Meltzer 85)

A second physical alteration was the loss of language and the freedom to use native language. Loss of language can be quite disconcerting as anyone who has traveled to a foreign speaking country can attest. An eleven year old boy was captured in Benin in 1745. In 1791, after purchasing his freedom in Philadelphia, Gustavus Vassa recorded his memories of the language barrier in his autobiography:

> The first object which saluted my eyes when I arrived on the coast was the sea, and a slave ship, which was then riding at anchor, and waiting for its cargo. These filled me with astonishment, which was soon connected with terror, when I was carried on board. I was immediately handled, and tossed up to see if I were sound, by some of the crew; and I was now persuaded that I had gotten into a world of bad spirits, and that they were going to kill me. Their complexions too differing so much from ours, their long hair, and the language they spoke (which was very different from any I had ever heard), united to confirm me in this belief . . . Soon after this

the other ship got her boats out, and they came on board of us, and the people of both ships seemed very glad to see each other. Several of the strangers also shook hands with us, African people, and made motions with their hands, signifying I suppose, we were to go to their country; but we did not understand them (Meltzer 3,7).

The use of African languages was disallowed at all times. Slaves learned American English as expediently as possible as they attempted to follow orders and avoid punishment.

Loss of family was particularly devastating as a sense of further isolation from familiar culture. Entire families were regularly parceled out to plantations far and near. In most cases separated families never saw their husbands, wives, children, or parents again. In Solomon Northrup's 1853 account of being on the slave auction block he described one woman's loss:

During the day, however, a number of sales were made. David and Caroline were purchased together by a Natchez planter. They left us, grinning broadly, and in a most happy state of mind, caused by the fact of their not being separated. Sethe was sold to a planter of Baton Rouge, her eyes flashing with anger as she was led away. The same man also purchased Randall. The little fellow was made to jump, and run across the floor, and perform many other feats, exhibiting his activity and condition. All the time the trade was going on, Eliza was crying aloud, and wringing her hands. She besought the man not to buy him, unless he also bought herself and Emily. She promised, in that case, to be the most faithful slave that ever lived. The man answered that he could not afford it, and then Eliza burst into a paroxysm of grief, weeping plaintively. Freeman turned round to her, savagely, with his whip in his uplifted hand, ordering her to stop her noise, or he would flog her. He would not have such work - - such sniveling; and unless she ceased that minute, he would take her to the yard and give her a hundred lashes. Yes, he would take the nonsense out of her pretty quick - - if he didn't might he be d------d. Eliza shrunk before him, and tried to wipe away her tears, but it was all in vain. She wanted to be with her children, she said, the little time she had to live. All the frowns and threats of Freeman could not wholly silence the afflicted mother. She kept on begging and beseeching them, most piteously, not to separate the three. Over and again she told them how she loved her boy. A great many times she repeated her former promises - - how hard she would labor day and night, to the last moment of her life; if he would only buy them all together. But it was of no avail; the man could not afford it. The bargain was agreed upon, and Randall must go alone. Then Eliza ran to him; embraced him passionately; kissed him again and again; told him to remember her - - all the while her tears falling in the boy's face like rain. Freeman damned her, calling her a blubbering, bawling wench, and ordered her to go to her place, and behave herself, and be somebody. He swore he wouldn't stand such stuff but a little longer. He would soon give her something to cry about, if she was not mighty careful, and that she might depend. The planter from Baton Rouge, with his new purchase, was ready to depart. "Don't cry, mama. I will be a good boy. Don't cry," said Randall, looking back, as they passed out of the door. What has become of the lad, God knows. It was a mournful scene indeed. I would have cried myself if I had dared. (Meltzer 87-88)

Loss of African identity also occurred in the form of re-naming. African cultural scholar Ihechukwu Madubuike pronounces, "Colonization as a system worked on the principle that everything African was primitive, barbarous, unholy. Everything from Europe, on the other hand, was pure and proper—civilized. Every effort was made to make Africans reject their own civilization and to look down on things African. To answer a white man's name was seen as one of the ways to becoming civilized, that is white" (11). Thus, an African named Omoro Kinte became Thomas Van

Renselaer. This alteration was not a minor change for Africans. According to Madubuike:

> Many Africans believe that the name a person bears is sometimes a key to the understanding of his character and behavior. . . To the African man in diaspora the knowledge of African names is invaluable. A detailed study of those aspects of his name which haven't been lost under the traumatic experience of slavery could give clues to what part of Africa the individual came from. In the South of the United States of America some Africans still have Essi, Ebi, and Ada as their names or parts of their names. These names which have survived cultural subjugation carry four centuries of history behind them, and a close analysis of them could reveal abundant facts hitherto unknown to other disciplines. (9)

Culturally speaking, loss of name equals loss of history and identity. Loss of history and, thus, identity results in identity-confusion. Regina Jennings, from Rutgers University's department of African American Studies, elaborates, "The practice of (re)naming a people already named kills off historical memory, and in this linguistic rupture avenues of defeat, inferiority, and sub-humanity find fields for repetition and proliferation" in her article "From Nigger to Negro: Dysfunctional Beginnings of Identity for New World Africans" (Azibo 251).

Finally, loss of lifestyle and lifestyle choices, further served to erase cultural history and identity. Every aspect of a slave's life was determined by his owner and the societal restrictions in which his owner lived. Where a slave could go, when a slave could go, what a slave could eat, when he could eat, what a slave could learn, what a slave could say, was determined and enforced without his consideration. Life on the plantation followed the dictates of the slave holders.

> All de slaves had dere gardens on my marster's plantation. He made dem do it, and dey liked it . . . In warm weather we had cotton clothes and in cold weather we had woolen clothes dat our marster had made fer us by de old ladies on de plantation. Isiah Jeffries. (Rawick 18)

The Negro Act of 1740, enacted in Charleston, South Carolina and quickly adopted by other slave-holding states, among other civil liberty bans, prohibited slaves from drumming. Drumming, an African form of celebration, communication, and ritual, was forbidden for fear that it might lead to insurrection like the revolt lead by Angolan slave Jemmy in 1739.

Instead, slaves learned European-influenced and American forms of rhythmic expression. Knowles writes, "As they struggled to adapt to their new surroundings, slaves were often forced to accept these European [dance] forms. Ex-slave Henry D. Jenkins recounted his memories of entertainment on the plantation :

> Dances? Yes sir, I can hear them fiddles and de pattin' now. Dis de way de dance was called: 'Balance all; sashshay to your partners; swing her 'round and promenade all; forward on de head; ladies change;' and all dat. Then de jigs went on. Believe me, them was times! (Rawick 25).

Slaves, for the most part, were only permitted to enjoy (real or shammed) these foreign forms of entertainment when it so pleased their owners. Christmas holidays, the master's entertainment of guests, or the master's personal enjoyment provided the occasions for slave performance of approved forms of diversion. An anonymous elderly ex-slave from Virginia recorded these memories in 1930:

> But soon arter a visitor come an' Marsa called Charlie to de house to show off what he knew. Marsa say, "Come here, Charlie, an' sing some rhymes fo' Mr. Henson." Don't know no new ones, Marsa," Charlie answered. "Come on, you African rascal, give me a rhyme fo' my company—one he ain't heard." (Meltzer 47)

Slaveholders made nearly every lifestyle choice for their slaves. The anonymous slave account mentioned above retells:

Marsa used to sometimes pick our wives fo' us. If he didn't have on his place enough women for the men, he would wait on de side of de road till a big wagon loaded with slaves come by. Den Marsa would stop de ole nigger-trader and buy you a woman. Wasn't no use tryin' to pick one, cause Marsa wasn't gonna pay but so much for her. All he wanted was a young healthy one who looked like she could have children, whether she was purty or ugly as sin. Den he would lead you an' de woman over to one of de cabins and stan' you on de porch. He wouldn't go in. No Sir. He'd stan' right dere at de do' an' open de Bible to de first thing he come to an' read sumpin real fast out of it. Den he close up de Bible an' finish up wid dis verse:

Dat you' wife
Dat you' husban'
I'se you' Marsa
She you' missus
You married. (Meltzer 46-47)

Loss of identity, through re-naming, lack of freedom in lifestyle choices, dress, dance, religion, language, food, and music, results in a psychological and physical dependence on the dominant culture as a source of replacement. As stated earlier, identification is the process whereby individuals form a self-identity. Eighteenth and nineteenth century African Americans, through force and compliance, identified, at least outwardly, with White America. Identification serves to increase the feelings of worth and importance by taking on the characteristics, values, or cultural attributes of some person or group that is well received by others. According to Azibo identification is psychologically essential for the ego development and maintenance of the individual or group.

The dilemma for African Americans during the birth of cultural formation is the fact that White America, as a whole, did not embrace or value African America. According to Phinney's theory on ethnic identity, particularly regarding the notion that an individual's self-concept stems from his knowledge of membership in a group and the sense of shared values and attitudes, African Americans could not avoid the eventual realization that there was a critical disconnect between their identification with White American values and their perceptions of the lack of identification White America felt toward them. Considering the explication of self-identity as a positive wish-fulfillment that reaches self-discovery largely through others, we can see how a mass African American identity crisis was born. Provided with Phinney's assertion that self-identity inherently seeks to be enhanced through positive reinforcement from a primary referent group, it becomes clear that positive self-identity for African Americans under the dominant influence, social and artistic, of White America may not easily be achieved.

"Self-concept," according to Allen's definition, is the result of the formation of self-identity. Establishing a clear, true self-concept became problematic for African Americans as a consequence of identification confusion from a negative projection of all things African. Hence, many slaves came to believe that they were naturally lazy or worthless as a race.

But it was the covert formation and maintenance of an African American group identity that fostered and fed the self-esteem of slaves and fueled the ongoing need to establish a cultural basis in the United States. Phinney defined group identity as an aspect of an individual's self-concept that stems from knowledge of his or her membership in a group and the significance attached to that membership, the sense of shared values and attitudes, and the awareness of behaviors, values, and history of the group. Racism was the grand design to fragment and subordinate the African American race but it also served to rally African Americans toward self-preservation because it formed the basis for common goals.

Membership in a pan African collective with a sense of shared values and attitudes became possible, and indeed, critical for Africans immediately upon captivity. At the height of the trade, European Slavers captured African men, women, and children heavily from the West African ports of Senegal, Cote d' Voire (Ivory Coast), The Gambia, Benin, Guinea, Ghana (then known as the Gold Coast), Sierra Leone, Guinea-Bissau, and as far away as Mozambique, Angola, and South Africa. However, according to Davidson, " . . . the main impact of the trade was felt on the southern side of this 'watershed [just below Senegal]' and it is there, near the coast and along the coast that one must look for its principal effects" (107). Even in such a relatively small area of trade hundreds of languages and dialects were spoken by the Mande people of the Guinea coast, known as Mandingos, the Yoruba people of western Nigeria, known as the Nagos, the Fon people of Dahomey, the Susu, known as the Xoxo, the Bambara, known as the Bambura of Middle Niger, the Tuculor, known as the Tucuxui of Senegal, the Wolofs of Senegal, the Kissi and the Senufu of Liberia, the Ibo of eastern Nigeria, the Fanti and the Ashanti of Ghana, and the Mandinka tribe of The Gambia, to name a few. In Gambia, people of one Mandinka tribe had difficulty comprehending the language of another Mandinka tribe in villages just ten miles away. Communication between the many tribes during the middle passage was often difficult, however, each captive was bound to one another through their common plight and common ancestry.

Gustavus Vassa wrote about his capture from Benin as a young boy:

> When I looked round the ship too and saw a large furnace or copper boiling, and a multitude of African people of every description chained together, every one of their countenances expressing dejection and sorrow, I no longer doubted of my fate; and, quite overpowered with horror and anguish, I fell motionless on the deck and fainted. . . In a little time after, amongst the poor chained men, I found some of my own nation, which in a small degree gave ease to my mind. (Meltzer 4-5)

Alex Haley's well-researched book *Roots* called a "historical novel" by sociology and anthropology professor Peter I. Rose (23), which tells the story of his actual family lineage from The Gambia to post-slavery America, illustrates this point. The purpose of using fiction here is to further depict the setting with as much detail as possible. Although a few factual accounts are available, such as the published journal entries of Gustavus Vassa (*The Interesting Narrative of the Life of Olaudah Equiano or Gustavas Vassa, the African)*, or Harriet A. Jacobs' autobiography *Life of a Slave Girl*, Haley compiled the existing historical evidence into a more richly detailed enactment of life from the slaveship to the slave plantation. The details in Haley's work based on an educated assessment of probabilities are the elements, which allow a keener insight into the mental machinations of the Africans in their fight to retain a group identity.

In the epic docu-story his Mandinkan great-great-great-great grandfather, Kunta Kinte made the middle passage to America in 1766 and Haley gives a quite probable narration of communication below deck on a slaveholding ship:

After a while, he heard near his right ear a low mutter. *"Jula?"* Kunta's heart leaped. He knew very little of the Wolof tongue, but he did know that Wolof and some others used the word *jula* to mean travelers and traders who were usually Mandinkas. And twisting his head a bit closer to the Wolof's ear, Kunta whispered, *"Jula. Mandinka."* For moments, as he lay tensely, the Wolof made no return sound. It went flashing through Kunta's head that if he could only speak many languages, as his father's brothers did . . . The steady murmuring that went on in the hold whenever the toubob were gone kept growing in volume and intensity as the men began to communicate better and better with one another. Words not understood were whispered from mouth to ear along the shelves until someone who knew more than one tongue would send back their meanings. In the process, all of the men along each shelf learned new words in tongues they had not spoken before. Sometimes men jerked upward, bumping their heads, in the double excitement of communicating with each other and the fact that it was being done without the toubob's knowledge. Muttering among themselves for hours, the men developed a deepening sense of intrigue and of brotherhood. Though they were of different villages and tribes, the feeling grew that they were not from different peoples or places. . . . One debate was suddenly interrupted when the voice of an elder rang out, "Hear me! Though we are of different tribes and tongues, remember that we are the same people! We must be as one village, together in this place!" (165-170)

So, how did African American culture survive the systematic de-Africanization process that attempted to alienate them from self-knowledge through a nihilistic stripping of identity to evolve into a rich African American-infused tradition with an ongoing drive to maintain itself in all facets of American life? Several factors facilitated the evolution. One key factor was the 100 years of ongoing legal slave trading. Until the international slave trade was banned in 1807, newly captured Africans arrived in America in a constant flow. New slaves brought fresh reminders of the homeland, which served to perpetuate African culture on the plantations. Another factor was the conscious and/or unconscious retention of African tradition.

The initial success of African America's efforts to maintain an awareness of its cultural behaviors, values, and history is a direct legacy of the cornerstone of African culture--oral/performance tradition. Denied freedom of African speech, the freedom of uncensored American speech, and the use of reading and writing, slaves relied heavily on the practices of their ancestors—the use of the body through storytelling, song, and even dance whenever possible, to communicate feelings and to convey information. Knowles writes, "The most primitive of all instruments, the human body, became the main source of rhythm and communication" (39).

Is it necessary for African Americans to keep its African American group-identity alive in pursuit of an ever-improving self-identity and heightened self-esteem? Does the collective memory of a distant continent have any bearing on a new identity forged from a subversive will to assert itself in a hostile society? Allen responds affirmatively to both queries by stating, "Many scholars have overlooked the contributions of African culture [in African American culture]. That is, the difference between African American culture and European culture and the retention of many aspects of African culture by African Americans has enabled African American culture to remain intact. . . This struggle to retain, restore, and reassert African culture continues over time with varying levels of success, which underscores the importance of the dynamic nature of the African self-concept" (55). Abolitionist Frederick Douglass wrote about his awareness of his relationship to Africa in an 1845 autobiography:

> The appalling darkness faded away, and I was master of the subject. There were slaves here, direct from Guinea; and there were many who could say that their fathers and mothers were stolen from Africa—forced from their homes, and compelled to serve as slaves. This, to me, was knowledge; but it was a kind of knowledge which filled me with a burning hatred of slavery, increased my suffering, and left me without the means of breaking away from my bondage. Yet it was knowledge quite worth possessing. (Meltzer 67-68).

In addition to retaining cultural memory, the task at hand for African America has historically been to reinstate its own culture as primary referent group; to replace the imposed images and aesthetics of White America with its own images and aesthetics. The early pioneering efforts of The African Grove Company, playwrights like Mr. Brown, William Wells Brown, Joseph P. Cotter, Edward Sheldon, Willis Richardson, Pauline Elizabeth Hopkins, and scholars like Frederick Douglass, W.E.B. du Bois, James Baldwin, Alain Locke, who all campaigned for a shift in cultural focus during and following slavery. However diverse the tactics have been, the over-arching focal point was and is the common goal of the group which positions African American society as a cultural collective. The shift in cultural focus was two-fold. The first intention was to shift African American consciousness from the need to seek approval and validation from Whites. In a 1963 interview for the *Paris Review* Ralph Ellison claimed, "Too many books by Negro writers are addressed to a white audience. By doing this the authors run the risk of limiting themselves to the audience's presumptions of what a Negro is or should be; the tendency is to become involved in polemics, to plead the Negro's humanity" (Adoff 89). The shift in African American focus was no easy task as the existence of Africans in America had been predicated on strict adherence to White America's sensibilities in all aspects of life. Physical and economic survival depended upon assimilation into White culture. Loften Mitchell discussed African Americans' complicity in racist attitudes in stating, "Many African Americans were also unaware of the stereotypes created by such comedians [Amos and Andy]. Brilliant men and women have reported that, when they heard these comics, they laughed, not realizing the humor was directed at *them*" (95). Of course, what is evident today in African American identity is significantly evolved from the early developmental years and will be comprehensively addressed in Chapter Five. The focus, at this point in time, is to understand the process of evolution and how the end result, or the present result, might be compromised in light of past efforts.

Mr. Brown and his African Grove Company, however, produced theatre for African Americans with a White seating section to appease protesters. The problem is that the protesters jeered, spit, shouted, cursed, and derided the actors and the productions. Audiences were outraged that the company would dare to put on productions by, for, and about African Americans. The theatre came under repeated attack by city officials. Every effort was made to shut down the space and the company through building inspection closings, fire marshal closings, disruptions of shows, and riots.

At the outset of the century, the rise of African American theatres faced a more civilized White hostility. African American performers began to reject the minstrel and vaudeville roles that were created, at the expense of dignity, to entertain Whites. African American performers who remained in the minstrel/vaudeville/burlesque scene began to abandon the elements, like blackface, that ridiculed African American culture. William Archer revealed, "During the first decade of the twentieth century, Black performers were exiled from the downtown theatres; so, they moved uptown to the Harlem playhouses" (10). Actually, there were no playhouses as such. Theatre spaces were created from converted libraries, social halls, and other available buildings. Exile to Harlem proved to be a blessing in disguise as performers and writers began to develop productions and audiences that were African American-oriented. Archer states, "All elements of the Black theatre were together for the first time in the Harlem theatres—actors, writers, musicians, dancers, and producers" (11). The Harlem renaissance of the 1920s and 1930s exploded with African American talent and for the first time in history, a true African American theatre ethic became established.

The second major shift in cultural focus was the intention to create a world, in art and business, with viable African American representatives; that is, creating a world where African Americans could see themselves reflected in dignified roles. Excluding literature, theatre, more than any other medium, has been the most groundbreaking in this regard, which is perhaps due to the fact that grass-roots efforts require little capital in comparison with radio, television, and film. Unfortunately, radio, television, and film attract mass audiences, while theatre is still under-populated. The need for African American representation in a representative world for self-reflective purposes is strong. Its absence leaves the African American population with few points of cultural reference, which in turn, runs the risk of primary group referent confusion. It is particularly necessary for African Americans to see themselves in culturally specific roles as a means of enhancing self-image and increasing cultural education. It is often presumed that African Americans hold information about African and African American culture by virtue of their skin color. In truth, public and most private education is still primarily provided from a White American account and African Americans learn as much about their heritage as Whites if exposure is not provided at home. Although the greatest developmental curve in African American identity occurred in the period between the late 19th and mid 20th centuries, it seems clear from the ongoing discourse on race and theatre that much work lies ahead. Evidence for this assertion is found in the writings of journalists like Kip Lee, who in his article "Evolution and Opinions of a Newjack" (2000) for the online publication, EON, reflects on the internal (self-induced) factors that inhibit a positive African American identity: "Once one knows our true history, it is difficult to understand how on earth our people could possibly be in the condition that we are presently confronted with. We have been so raped of identity, land and history that we are ourselves lost in a void of self concept and self development . . . The strong desire to assimilate has provided for the weakening of our own Black institutions" (2). Clearly there are still identity problems to be resolved in African American society in today's world. Fostering a conscious cultural identity for African Americans requires specific (in relation to African American cultural life) representation in all fields, including theater.

Chapter Five

CONCLUSION: SOME SOLUTIONS

We have seen that the theoretical, practical, and political struggle over color blind casting has left theatre practitioners at an impasse. It is also clear that emotions and artistic investments run very high around the issue. We have seen that African American cultural and social development has followed a path of self-definition with aims apart from White American culture and that African American identity concerns need to be more fully considered when weighing the use of this practice. Also shown is the fact that there is an imbalance in the number of African American theatres in America as well as an imbalance in being able to use color blindness in the reverse – color blind casting projects have primarily used African American artists in White roles. It is clear that a resolution depends upon balancing out the needs of the two parties who are considered in this treatment. Finally, we know that this is a debate that will not resolve itself without much concerted effort. Many scholars have put a good deal of thought into workable solutions. William Sun believes " . . . that politically, in the United States, there are and should be some rules in the area of acting across ethnic lines" (94). Sun, in his 2000 article "Power and Problems of Performance across Ethnic Lines" for *The Drama Review*, supports non-traditional casting practices and the use of blackface (or other color-changing make up) as a means of honoring other cultures while recognizing the need to use such practices in the right context and with great sensitivity. He distinguishes his non-traditionalist position from that of other non-traditionalists like Richard Schechner and Leslie Radford, whom he calls "universalists" that "promotes a humanist's color-blind approach to theatre based on the belief that race and ethnicity, along with gender, are relative after all . . . anything goes, any direction is OK" (86). Jacqueline Lo and Helen Gilbert suggest that our "increasingly hybridized" society should, like "border art," strive to push the boundaries with non-traditional (specifically, cross-cultural) theatre and laid out a model towards that end (49). To my knowledge, no models or prescriptions for reducing the use of color blind practices has been written, although, as seen earlier, many African Americans have offered informal suggestions. My proposals are based on those suggestions and on the views of some scholars and practitioners who are non-traditionalists.

Of the three choices allowable to us – all color blind casting, no color blind casting, or some combination of color blind casting -- imagining a world with all color blind theatre is not a practical option. It would lead us into the very situation that August Wilson and other African American practitioners have rallied to avoid – an absence of culturally specific theatre. Attempting to eliminate all color blind theatre is equally unthinkable. Dramas that might allow for inter-cultural, equal representation would never be written and staged. Segregated theatre would help create the society that Robert Brustein and others are determined to avoid – a regressed civilization. Additionally, in light of the ever-growing interracial population in America, bi-racial individuals could find themselves caught between African American and White American theatre without a home for artistic expression. Many would not consider either of the above options.

The third choice, a combination of color blind, mainstream, and ethnic theatre in America, is already in operation. However, it is a result of individual artistic prerogative rather than mutual support and cooperation toward a common vision. Combining efforts to consciously direct the use of what appears to be the most favorable option is a responsibility that we, as American theatre artists must shoulder. In that vein, the following ideas are offered as general guidelines when beginning the process of using this third choice of a combination of color blind and culturally specific theatre in a mutually supportive way. I would preface the following guidelines by saying that we should try to incorporate actors of all backgrounds into suitable roles and use drama that includes many cultural backgrounds. Such drama not only mirrors large parts of our society, but also helps influence the direction of society towards a more inclusionary world.

The first step in being mutually responsible citizens is to begin to use language that is accurate and useful for more effectual communication. The term "color blind" connotes a refusal to see color, which Harry Newman hoped would evolve into an inability to see color – a disablement of mental perception. Newman envisioned non-traditional casting as a conscious conditioning process that would reprogram the mind over time. As quoted earlier, "We called ourselves a 'project' because we hoped (and hope) to be short-lived, to act as a catalyst for change, rather than become an institution interested primarily in self-perpetuation. . . . In time we hope that – like our organization – the phrase itself will disappear, and 'non-traditional' casting will become the performing arts' new tradition" (Newman 24). The two significant problems with Newman's aspirations for non-traditional casting and by extension, color blind casting, are that color can never be erased from the mind and far from disappearing, the phrase has mushroomed to enormous proportions. Use of the term has become problematic. To complicate matters further, much of what is labeled color blind theatre is in actuality color-conscious. The contradictions point to the futility in using such language. Newman was aware of its limitations. "Although there are drawbacks to the phrase [non-traditional casting], we at the NTCP adopted it as part of our title because it had already gained a measure of currency in the industry and because it seemed provocative" (24). It may be some time before we, as Americans, settle on workable terms for communication. Rodney Douglas' term "mixed race casting" is awkward, yet accurate and will serve for the purposes of this conclusion.

The second step toward resolution is deciding when and where such casting should occur in the most conscientious and appropriate way. There are cases where casting African Americans in the classics (conceptual casting) carries great meaning and enhancement. There are also cases where the entire world of a classic placed in an African American setting with a African American cast can carry great resonance also. In these cases, careful consideration should be given to the aims of such casting and to weighing out the benefits for all (including audience members). We should avoid reverse race casting that is not conceptual. If an all White cast of actors performed August Wilson's play *Jitney* in Black dialect and manner, the uproar would be great. African American actors performing in White dialect and manner are equally unsettling. Generally speaking, casting individual African American actors or whole casts of African American actors in the works of Chekov, Ibsen, Shakespeare, and other dramas written by, about, and for non-African Americans is socially and culturally remiss. Mixed race casting should always be used to honor all artists involved. If the cultural heritage of an actor, beyond skin color, cannot be factored into a production, there is very little value (talent notwithstanding) in using that particular actor beyond artistic and social provocation. African American actor Tico Wells concurs, stating, "Every time you see one Black person in a show or one Asian person or an interracial cast, unless the piece is saying something to mankind, unless the director has some kind of vision and is pooling the inner sources of these talented people then it's just a coloring book of colors and not necessarily anything of substance" (Davis and Newman 103). The "inner sources" that Wells speaks of are more than just performance skills, they are the cultural make-up of an ethnic actor beyond skin color. We are performing a greater disservice to the evolution of society by communicating a disregard (albeit with honorable intentions) for one another's cultural heritage (speech, mannerisms, etc.). This is only to say that an actor is, in part, defined by his or her cultural heritage and one's heritage cannot and should not be ignored onstage. Henry Miller of the American Folk Theatre states, "When are we not going to try to get Blacks to pretend that they are something other than they are?" (Davis and Newman 58). Paul Robeson, Jr. quotes writer James Baldwin as saying:

> The popular culture is designed to make money. Therefore, the popular culture confronted with a Paul Robeson has to find a way to make him moving, charming, noble, innocent, but above all irrelevant. It wants to present him as a kind of chocolate John Wayne. This is based on the murderous assumption that I want to be like Ronald Reagan. That I really believe that the cowboy who murdered the Indian is a hero and will save my life. (Davis and Newman 66-67)

Baldwin was accusing mainstream theatre of portraying African American artists as mere White counterparts without regard for their true heritage. Of course, cultural heritage is not determined by skin color. One cannot say that every African American relates to the same customs, values, and mores. Environment and experience also greatly influence one's cultural reference points. But having derived from generally similar backgrounds – African and early American – African Americans, as a whole, tend to carry common traditions and customs. Africa has many varied countries and people, however, the bulk of captives came from the western region where an overlapping of tradition, language, food, and ritual practices was the basis of their commonalities. Likewise, the bulk of slaves in America were deposited in the southeastern states and only filtered to the north en masse in the early 20th century. The fact that most African Americans followed the same basic roads until less than 100 years ago leads to the conclusion that, in general, they share similar reference points. In terms of collective identity, Richard Allen reported that sociologists " . . . Porter and Washington (1993) also observed that the available research indicates that most African-Americans have high group identity, and that while differences across certain classes have been reported, such differences have been inconsistent" (91). Here, having high group identity means identification to a great degree.

In honoring the heritage of all artists we might consider producing dramatic works that are written to specifically include different cultural groups or written to allow for the portrayal of different cultural groups. One example is Israel Horowitz' allegorical play *Line* about five individuals waiting in line. The only related characters are Molly and Arnall. In my production of the drama at the University of Missouri, I took the liberty of casting the couple interracially (East Indian and White American) because of the reality of such a real life representation, the universality of the play's message and given circumstances, and because of the campus setting within which I was directing. In honoring all cultures, I asked the East Indian actor to play his role as an East Indian rather than as a White male or racially-neutral character as is often the case. His accent, inflections, mannerisms, and dress were culturally specific and brought greater dimension to the production. The question may be raised, "Who determines what counts for universality in a play's meaning?" The playwright's given circumstances in the drama and the director's recognition of universal themes will determine how a play might be used in color blind ways. Caution should be exercised in using White American dramas with universal themes for the casting of African American actors. Plays such as Arthur Miller's *Death of a Salesman* carries a universal theme of hope and despair with no particular given circumstances pointing to race. However, a director or producer should consider how the language, speech patterns, and other seemingly minor considerations like character names can be more reflective of a White author's cultural references rather than an African American's cultural references. Twentieth and twenty-first century African Americans do not generally speak as the character Ben speaks, "William, you're being first-rate with your boys. Outstanding, manly chaps!" or name their sons "Biff." In disregarding these details a color blind production could run the risk of sounding like a parody.

The question of where mixed-race casting should be utilized is also critical. The university setting is where many practitioners suggest the need for and the appropriateness of mixed race casting. Academia is where learning often begins for young practitioners. It is also where the aspirations of Harry Newman and the NTCP can be nurtured. Richard Schechner states, "Many acting classes—needing to exercise all the students enrolled regardless of race, gender, etc.—employ the mixed cast technique" (5). The ability to accept and include cultural others can be fostered in a learning environment like college institutions. Excluding African American students (or excluding African American drama for that matter) from college campus productions sends a potent message to White American students about cultural inclusion, to African American students about the importance of their development as an artist of color, and to the community at large about who and what is important in art. If students of color cannot find academic and artistic expression in university theatre departments, they will lose interest in the program, perhaps in theatre. How can we, as Americans, foster more African American talent on the professional stage if we are not professionally training them at the college level? Douglas Turner Ward stated," In a university context when you see a play cast with a 17 year old Oakie girl as Lady Macbeth and the Black 17 year old girl is not cast, neither one is right for it. Why do you exclude the Black from the cast?" (Davis and Newman 20). But universities should not stop at the simple inclusion of African Americans and other minorities in the production of the classics, and the Albee, O'Neill, Chekov, and Ionesco plays. Universities ought to include the Hansberry, Wilson, Shange, Childress, and Cleage dramas, as well. Placing White students in African American plays can provide valuable acting experiences and sensitivity training. James Earl Jones offers his view stating:

> Some of the most exciting times I had as a student (I still am a student) were the chances I had to play a woman, to play Native American, to play Caucasian. Now, I think on that level of students and workshops, it is a very important American experience. We learn more about how other people think, feel and are, really are. (Davis and Newman 76)

Although it is not an original idea, I would suggest that the practice of using the college setting as an exploration of ethnic and mixed race productions needs to occur more often than has been the case. University theatre departments may be concerned about presenting mixed race and African American dramas because of an insufficient African American student body. In 1985 when the University of Missouri department of theatre allocated funds for a Black Theatre Workshop project, there were only 3 African American students in an undergraduate and graduate program of approximately 200 majors. Because the Black Theatre Workshop staged plays like Charles Fuller's *A Soldier's Play* and Lorraine Hansberry's *A Raisin in the Sun*, the workshop project grew over a three year period to approximately 25 African students from many other departments – including business and law students. As a result the department of theatre gained new majors from other departments and incoming students. Additionally, the community, African American and White American, came out to see these non-typical campus productions, which increased department revenue, and many campus-wide students became a part of the arts. The Black Theatre Workshop at the University of Missouri's department of theatre went on to win national grants and recognition and showcased at Lincoln Center in New York and at the Royal Shakespeare Company's theatre in London. One of the workshop members, previously an economics major, wrote the original script that brought the group its national and international recognition. The overriding conclusion is that if we present it, they will come.

A third step in using mixed race casting responsibly is to ensure that a balance between all types of theatre is maintained in America. It calls for correcting any existing imbalances. The most well-known imbalance is, of course, the disproportionate number of African American LORT theatres. Crossroads Theatre in New Brunswick, New Jersey is the only African American LORT theatre amongst 66 LORT theatres nationally. Zelda Fichlander, artistic director of the graduate acting program at NYUs Tisch School of the Arts challenged America thusly:

> Is it not a thought worth considering, by one or a consortium of foundations and/or in collaboration with the NEA, to set aside a sizeable pot of money (as a sizeable pot was recently set aside to assist our mainstream theatres in achieving greater

audience diversity), expressly to give a leg up to a number of struggling Black theatres (or other ethnically specific groups), some of them like Karmu House of long standing and contribution? ("On Cultural Power" 57).

Woodie Allen King, Jr., producing director of the New Federal Theatre in New York echoed Fichlander's sentiments:

> Given the situation – that of the 66 LORT theaters, only one can be considered a Black theatre – what is to be done? Create a new not-for-profit 501©3 institution at $5 or $6 million per year? Or enhance the budgets of 10 of the oldest Black theatres across the U.S.? It seems to me that foundations and other funding sources could get a bigger bang for their buck if they enhanced New Federal Theatre in New York, National Black Theatre in New York, Billie Holiday Theatre in Brooklyn, Jomandi Theatre in St. Louis, Ensemble Theatre in Houston, Lorraine Hansberry Theatre in San Francisco, ETA Theatre in Chicago, Penumbra in Minneapolis and the New Freedom Theatre in Philadelphia. All of these theatres are more than 15 years old; some will be celebrating their 30th year in the year 2000. For each of these theatres to be included in the membership of LORT, it would cost an additional $400,000 per year. That would enable the theatres to increase fees to playwrights, directors, actors, designers and staff. It would further help these institutions set up subscription drives and development offices. Marketing and promotion would be on par with other LORT theatres. Full-time production managers and company managers could be hired to oversee productions and deal with artists. ("On Cultural Power" 15, 59)

Sufficient funding for African American theatres would also allow new playwriting talent to be explored which was of particular importance to many African American practitioners who attended the 1986 NTCP Symposium. A call for more African American dramatic material would assist in keeping the balance between non-traditional, mainstream and ethnic theatre. Some practitioners, like Robert Brustein, are concerned that such theatres do not sustain themselves and that African American theatre will forever be beholden to White American funding. There is much that can be said (outside of the scope of this work), regarding who truly owns and has rights to the funding that is generated by federal and private agencies, but suffice it to say, without the funds to implement a sustainable plan, African American theatres cannot progress to that point. Building and supporting African American theatre is not a fruitless endeavor. Allen quotes scholar S. Amin saying, "Many people find it exceedingly difficult to see Blacks [in America] as controllers of their own fate and builders of enduring civilizations" (19). African Americans are less apprehensive. Woodie King Jr. states in *Impact of Race: Theatre and Culture*, "Black businesses sustain themselves because they have a product that Black people need. Black artists create the spiritual and cultural nourishment Black people need" (14). Again, if we create it (the drama, the buildings, and the outreach), they will come. Douglas Turner Ward states, "There has to be an inclusion – a wider inclusion, first and foremost of Black material in which the presence of Black people will be a natural part of the artistic project. Then you can start to talk about everything else" (Davis and Newman 20).

To summarize, the plan that is suggested to address African American needs, to balance out existing situations, and to make use of what Lieberman calls an "enormously appealing and compelling" idea, entails the following changes:

a) Consider new intercultural/mixed race projects that represent the African American race with all of its cultural expressions rather than merely the Black color.

b) Encourage mixed race casting experimental practices *and* ethnic theatre at learning institutions.

c) Increase the support for national African American theatre and drama.

d) Avoid casting African Americans in White European and American classics without a conceptual base for representing that actor and his/her culture onstage.

e) Avoid reverse race productions that are not cross-cultural.

These are all preliminary steps toward making appropriate use of a practice that is not without its merits. Mixed race casting allows practitioners to assist society in imagining a multi-representation of cultures, to impact world views, and it allows for collaboration through balanced artistic cultural exchange. Its merits have also been diminished by a tendency to only superficially represent cultural others by way of skin color without allowing racial heritage to blossom. It should also be noted these suggestions may need to be revisited and revised down the road, always leaving the door open for new insights arising from new social developments. As we begin another decade searching for ways to further establish communication regarding race in theatre, we should reflect on the words of Zelda Fichlander who stated, "Peace among cultures is only possible if we can recognize the Other as different and valuable and interesting in that difference" ("On Cultural Power" 57). I would add that we should also make every effort to move beyond recognition into action.

WORKS CITED

Adoff, Arnold, ed. Black on Black: Commentaries by Negro Americans. New York: The Macmillan Company, 1968.

Allen, Richard L. The Concept of Self: A Study of Black Identity and Self Esteem. Detroit: Wayne State University Press, 2001.

Archer, Leonard C. Black Images in the American Theatre. New York: Pageant-Poseidon. 1973.

Azibo, Daudi Ajani ya, Ed. African-Centered Psychology: Culture-Focusing for Multicultural Competence. Durham, NC: Carolina Academic Press, 2003.

Berry, Ralph. "Shakespeare and Integrated Casting." Contemporary Review 285 (July 2004): 35-39.

Bond, Frederick W. The Negro and the Drama: The Direct and Indirect Contribution Which the American Negro Has Made to Drama and the Legitimate Stage, with the Underlying Conditions Responsible. Washington, D.C.: McGrath Publishing Company, 1969.

Brown, Michael K., Martin Carnoy, Elliott Currie, Troy Duster, David B. Oppenheimer, Marjorie M. Shultz, and David Wellman. Whitewashing Race: The Myth of a Color-Blind Society. Berkeley: University of California Press, 2003.

Brustein, Robert. "Subsidized Racism." American Theatre. 14 (October 1996): 26-27, 100-104.

Carson, Clayborne, Garrow, David J., Gill, Gerald, Harding, Vincent, Hine, Clark, eds. The Eyes on the Prize Civil Rights Reader. New York: Penguin Books, 1991.

"Color." Webster's New World Dictionary. College ed. 1958.

Curtis, Susan. The First Black Actors on the Great White Way. Columbia, Missouri: University of Missouri Press, 1998.

Davidson, Basil. The African Slave Trade: Precolonial History 1450-1850. Boston: Little, Brown and Company, 1961.

Davis, Clinton Turner, and Newman, Harry, eds. <u>Beyond Tradition</u>. New York: The Sarabande Press, 1988.

Miller, Arthur. <u>Death of a Salesman</u>. New York: Dramatists Play Service, 1948.

Douglas, Rodney K. <u>The Concept and Practice of Mixed Racial Casting in New York Theatres and Other Regions, 1960-1990</u>. Dissertation Abstracts International, Section A: The Humanities and Social Sciences, 2002 June; 62 (12): 3999. New York U, 2002.

Euba, Femi. <u>Archetypes, Imprecators, and Victims of Fate: Origins and Developments of Satire in African Drama</u>. New York: Greenwood Press, 1989.

Evans, G. Blakemore, ed. <u>Elizabethan-Jacobean Drama: The Theatre in its Time</u>. New York: New Amsterdam Books, 1990.

Fabre, Geneviève. <u>Drumbeats Masks and Metaphor: Contemporary Afro-American Theatre</u>. Cambridge, Massachusetts: Harvard University Press, 1983.

Gardner, Elysa. "Black Theater Examines State of the Art." <u>USA Today</u>. 3 August 2003. 29 March 2004 .

Gold, Sylviane. "Seeking a Theater Varied as a Rainbow." <u>New York Times</u>. 23 February 1997: sec. 2: 5.

Goodman, Gerald Thomas. <u>The Black Theatre Movement.</u> Diss. University of Pennsylvania, 1974. Ann Arbor: UMI, 1974. 7514566.

<u>Gorèe: Door of No Return</u>. Prod. Même Chose Production for the Humanities and Sciences. Videocassette. 1991.

Gossett, T. F. <u>Race: The History of an Idea in America</u>. Dallas: Southern Methodist University Press, 1963.

Guillory-Brown, Elizabeth. <u>Their Place on the Stage: Black Women Playwrights in America</u>. New York: Greenwood Press, 1988.

Haley, Alex. <u>Roots</u>. Garden City, New York: Doubleday & Company, Inc., 1974.

Hamalian, Leo and Hatch, James V., eds. <u>Lost Plays of the Harlem Renaissance 1920-1940</u>. Detroit: Wayne State University, 1996.

_____. The Roots of African American Drama: An Anthology of Early Plays, 1858-1938. Detroit: Wayne State University Press, 1991.

Harris, Joseph. E. Africans and Their History. New York: Mentro Books, 1987.

Hartigan, Patti. "Brustein, Wilson Tiff Obscures Real Issues." The Boston Globe, 4 October 1996: E3.

Haskins, James, Butts, Hugh F. The Psychology of Black Language. New York: Hippocrene Books, 1973.

Hatch, James V., ed. Black Theatre, U.S.A.: Forty-Five Plays by African Americans 1847-1974. New York: The Free Press, 1974.

Herskovits, Melville. The Myth of the Negro Past. Boston: Beacon Press, 1990.

Hill, Errol, ed. The Theater of Black Americans. 2 vols. Englewood Cliffs, New Jersey: Prentice-Hall, Inc., 1980.

Hulbert, Dan. "Wilson's Dramas No Longer Confined to Theater Stage." The Atlanta Journal and Constitution. 15 January 1997: O3B.

Keyssar, Helene. The Curtain and the Veil: Strategies in Black Drama. New York: Burt Franklin and Company, 1981.

King, Woodie, Jr. The Impact of Race: Theatre and Culture. New York: Applause, 2003.

Knowles, Mark. Tap Roots: The Early History of Tap Dancing. Jefferson, North Carolina: McFarland & Company, Inc., 2002.

Krasner, David. Resistance, Parody, and Double Consciousness in African American Theatre, 1895-1910. New York: St. Martin's Press, 1997.

Lee , Kip. "Evolutions and Opinions of a Newjack." EON 1996. 14 September 2000 .

Lieberman, Robert C. Shaping Race Policy: The United States in Comparative Perspective. New Jersey: Princeton University Press, 2005.

Litwack, Leon F. Been in the Storm So Long: The Aftermath of Slavery. New York: Vintage Books, 1979.

Lyman, Darryl. Great African-American Women. New York: Gramercy Books, 1999.

Madubuike, Ihechukwu. A Handbook of African Names. Washington, D.C.: Three Continents Press, 1976.

Mathabane, Mark. Kaffir Boy. New York: New American Library, 1986.

Meltzer, Milton. In Their Own Words: A History of the American Negro. New York: Thomas Y. Crowell Company, 1964.

Mitchell, Loften. Black Drama: The Story of the American Negro in the Theatre. New York: Hawthorn Books, Inc., 1967.

_____. Voices of the Black Theatre. Clifton, New Jersey: James T. White and Company, 1975.

Nesmith, Graham N. " Lloyd Richards: Reminiscence of a Theatre Life and Beyond." African American Review 18 (Fall 2005): 39:3.

Newman, Harry. "Holding Back: The Theatre's Resistance to Non-Traditional Casting." TDR. 33:3 (1989): 22-36.

Nunns, Stephen. "Wilson, Brustein, and the Press." American Theatre Journal. 14:3 March (1997): 18.

Oates, Stephen B. Let the Trumpet Sound: The Life of Martin Luther King, Jr. New York: New American Library, 1982.

"On Cultural Power." American Theatre Journal. May/June (1997): 14-17, 52-62.

Pao, Angela C. "Recasting Race: Casting Practices and Racial Formations." 41:2 Theatre Survey. (November 2000): 1-21.

Patterson, Orlando. "Being and Africanness." The New York Times. 8 January 2006. 29 March 2006 .

Phinney, Jean. S. "Ethnic Identity in Adolescents and Adults." vol. 108 Psychological Bulletin. (1990): 499-514.

_____. "Ethnic Identity and self-esteem: a review and integration." vol. 13 Hispanic Journal of Behavioral Science. (1991): 193-208.

"Race." <u>Webster's New World Dictionary</u>. College ed. 1958.

Rawick, George P., ed. <u>The American Slave: A Composite Autobiography</u>. vols. 2 and 3. Westport, Connecticut: Greenwood Publishing Company, 1941.

Rose, Peter I.. <u>They and We: Racial and Ethnic Relation in the United States</u>. New York: Random House, 1981.

Rosenberg, Morris. "Self-concept research: A historical overview." vol. 68 <u>Social Forces</u>. (1989): 34-44.

Rosenberg, Morris., Schooler, C., & Rosenberg, F. "Global Self-esteem and specific self-esteem: Different concepts, different outcomes." vol. 60 <u>American Sociological Review.</u> (1995): 141-156.

Schechner, Richard. "Race Free, Gender Free, Body-Type Free, Age Free Casting." 33:1 <u>The Drama Review</u>. (1989): 4-12.

"Self-esteem." <u>Webster's New World Dictionary</u>. College ed. 1958.

Seller, Maxine Schwartz, ed. <u>Ethnic Theatre in the United States</u>. Westport, Connecticut: Greenwood Press, 1983.

Sheppard, Jennifer L. "Theatrical Casting: Discrimination or Artistic Freedom." <u>Columbia-VLA Journal of Law and the Arts</u>. 15 (1991): 267-282.

Simonson, Robert. <u>Role of a Lifetime</u>. New York: Back Stage Books, 1999.

Sinkler, George. <u>The Racial Attitudes of American Presidents from Abraham Lincoln to Theodore Roosevelt</u>. New York: Doubleday Anchor Books, 1972.

Stampp, Kenneth M. <u>The Peculiar Institutution: Slavery in the Ante-Bellum South</u> New York: Vintage Books, 1956.

Sun, William H. "Power and Problems of Performance across Ethnic Lines: An Alternative Approach to Nontraditional Casting." 44: 4 <u>TDR</u>. (Winter 2000): 86-95.

Thompson, Ayanna. <u>Colorblind Shakespeare: New Perspectives on Race and Performance</u>. New York, Routledge, 2006.

Thompson, Debby. "Is Race a Trope?" <u>African American Review.</u> 12 Spring (2003): 27.

Turner, Lorenzo. <u>Africanisms in the Gullah Dialect</u>. An Arbor: The University of Michigan Press, 1973.

Wagner, Vit. "Wouldn't She Make a GREAT Hamlet?" <u>Toronto Star</u> 15 July 1995 final ed.: K3.

West, Cornel. <u>Race Matters</u>. Boston: Beacon Press, 1993.

White, Joseph L. <u>The Psychology of Blacks: An Afro-American Perspective</u>. New Jersey: Prentice-Hall, Inc., 1984.

Williams, Mance. <u>Black Theatre in the 1960s and 1970s: A Historical-Critical Analysis of the Movement</u>. Westport, Connecticut: Greenwood Press, 1985.

Williams, Patricia J. <u>Seeing a Color-Blind Future: The Paradox of Race</u>. New York: Noonday Press, 1997.

Wilson, August. "The Ground On Which I Stand." <u>American Theatre</u>. New York: Theatre Communications Group, 1nc

WORKS CONSULTED

Afro-American Poetry and Drama, 1760-1975: a Guide to Information Sources. Detroit: Gale, 1979.

Archer, Leonard C. Black Images in the American Theatre. New York: Pageant-Poseidon. 1973.

Effiong, Philip Uko. In Search of a Model for African-American Drama. New York: University Press of America, 2000.

Lo, Jacqueline, and Gilbert, Helen. "Toward Topography of Cross-Cultural Theatre Praxis." 46:3 The Drama Review. (Fall 2002): 31-53.

Molette, Carlton and Barbara. Black Theatre: Premise and Presentation. Bristol, Indiana: Wyndam Hall Press 1986.

Ogunbiyi, Yemi. New Black Playwrights in America (1960-1975): Essays in Theatrical Criticism. Diss. New York University, 1976. Ann Arbor: UMI, 1976. 7619529.

Olaniyan, Tejumola. Scars of Conquest/Masks of Resistance: The Invention of Cultural Identities in African, African-American, and Caribbean Drama. New York: Oxford University Press, 1995.

Sanders, Leslie Catherine. The Development of Black Theater in America. Baton Rouge: Louisiana State University Press, 1988.

Sheppard, Jennifer L. "Theatrical Casting: Discrimination or Artistic Freedom." Columbia-VLA Journal of Law and the Arts. 15 (1991): 267-282.

Singleton, Carole Waters. Black Theatre as Cultural Communication: An Educative Process. Diss. University of Maryland, 1975. Ann Arbor: UMI, 1975. 7529133.

Woll, Allen. Dictionary of the Black Theater: Broadway, Off-Broadway, and Selected Harlem Theater. Westport, CT: Greenwood, 1983.

About the Author

Dr. Jocelyn A. Brown is a writer and educator in the arts, particularly as they relate to African American issues. She has written numerous articles in the Arts and Entertainment field. Brown is a member of the National Scholars Honor Society and the National Educators Association. Brown's drama, *Doors: Dramatic Dialogue Between and About Blacks and Whites*, was awarded the outstanding new play of the year by a female writer in 1992 by the Zora Neale Hurston Workshop at the New Federal Theatre in New York City where it showcased in 1993. Brown is the author of *Lest We Forget,* a drama about youth in the civil rights movement, and *A Trip to the Zoo.* Currently, Brown is president and CEO of Writing Professional, a consulting firm (**http://writingprofessional.org**). For articles by or about Dr. Brown, please visit ezinearticles.com or writingprofessional.org

Printed in Great Britain
by Amazon